Learn

Psychology of Accelerated Learning Unfold

Genious Learning Techniques to Cut Your Learning Time in Half

2nd Edition

Jackson Keller

The trademarks that are used are without any consent, and the publication of the trademark is without permission or backing by the trademark owner.

All trademarks as well as brands within this book are for clarifying purposes only and are the owned by the owners themselves, not affiliated with this document.

Table of Contents

Introduction

As human beings, we are always learning new skills and additional information. Our brains are geared to constantly be adding to our store of knowledge. The data collected from our senses is filtered and analyzed based on what we already know about a specific topic. Our life experiences also play a part in how we analyze and classify or filter new information. The question for teachers, trainers and others within various organizations is how to maximize our brain's ability to take in new information and process it quickly. By doing so, organizations find that they can train their workers to execute new skills faster, thus saving time and money in the long run.

While we are always taking in new data, we might always understand what is being presented. Therefore, a critical part of learning any new skill or task is to be able to then execute the skill or task properly with minimal practice or additional training. There are those who spend their lives studying how we learn and then execute based on what we learn. These researchers have come up with an effective way to teach students, workers and even management through a process called Accelerated Learning.

But what is Accelerated Learning? What is involved in creating an Accelerate Learning program tailored to your needs or the needs of your company or school? In this book, we will explore Accelerated Learning, how it works and most importantly, how you can put it into practice by means of guideposts and other methods. So let's start by learning a bit more about what Accelerate Learning really is all about, particularly in terms of what it means for teachers and students.

Chapter One:
What is Accelerated Learning?

Many of us remember sitting in a classroom or training center at one time or another feeling completely lost. The teacher ends the session and asks if there are any questions. You feel as if you should raise your hand and ask if she or he can simply go over everything just one more time.

But why does that happen to us? For many, it happens more frequently than we are willing to admit. In large part, this occurs because the teaching method employed is not adaptable to the way we ourselves learn. Therefore, we spend a great deal of time taking information and attempting to translate it into a method we understand before we can even begin the task of processing the data and applying it.

Researchers have found, however, that human actually used some consistent methods to learn and analyze information. Consider them the natural reflexes of our brains. By tapping into these natural learning methods, researches have been able to create a means of increasing the speed and retention of students, employees and those within the management of any specific industry.

The reason that accelerated learning appears to be so successful is that it does not just involve one part of the body or one area of the brain. This method is all encompassing, involving creativity, physical activity, images and even music to help an individual drill down into their deeper learning potential. Individuals find themselves deeply drawn into the learning process, thus making what they are learning stick with them even better.

Yet to really get the most out of this type of learning method, one needs to have the type of environment that is conducive to accelerated learning. What is involved in the optimal environment? First and most important, the learning environment needs to be positive, providing the students with a can do feeling. If students feel stressed, unsafe or a lack of interest in the material, they will not truly benefit from the other areas of the learning method.

What are some ways to create this positive learning environment? Consider adding a stretching exercise or deep breathing to the beginning of a learning session to give students a chance to release their stress from the day prior to diving into the material. If the material is work related, it is important to inform your students early in the session about how they can personally benefit from the data being covered. This will allow you to peak their interest in the material. Creating interest for your students might vary depending on your audience and the material that is to be covered during the accelerated learning session.

Where are you holding the session itself? This will come into play if the area is considered unsafe. When students are concerned about their own safety or protecting their belongings, such as a purse or car, an instructor is not going to have their full attention. Optimal accelerated learning is not likely to take place as a result.

When an instructor takes in the emotional, physical and social environment of her students, she can find ways to tweak the learning environment to reflect a more positive student experience. Students who feel positive and invigorated to learn are now ready to maximize their own natural learning abilities to absorb these new skills or data.

By creating this type of learning environment, an instructor is attempting to engage the total student. Passive learning means that the student is not necessarily active in the process. Imagine a situation where you are just observing the actions of others without participating in the process. We can take a baking lesson as an example. While you might pick up some of the techniques involved in creating that beautiful cake or dessert, those who are able to participate in the process find themselves retaining more knowledge and gaining valuable experience.

Accelerated learning works on a similar ideal. Students are involved in the learning process, using activities that get them moving and thinking. Thus, presentation or material based learning experiences are typically avoided, because they can be less engaging for the students.

As our baking example also showcased, the best learning experiences are often a collaborative effort. Social interactions through group activities can assist in engaging those students who might otherwise be turned off due to a lack of interest in the topic or skill set to be mastered. When creating any lesson plan with accelerated learning at its core, it is critical to make sure the students are engaging, not only with the instructor, but with the other students. Learning collaboration involves the students with their instructor, but also with their fellow learners. Each individual student benefits from the strengths of the others as they take on a new skill set.

Another social aspect is the understanding that each individual has their own particular learning style. Often the variety of learning options, in terms of activities, can engage all of your students to their fullest levels. Instead of a one size fits all approach, accelerate learning focuses on creating a learner centered approach that encourages all students to engage their five senses completely.

With our baking example, our five senses play a key role in achieving the best results in terms of the final product. It would be improbable to create an amazing dessert if you cannot taste it, smell it or were unable to confirm that you were using the proper ingredients from sight. In much the same way, a learning experience needs to immerse a student's five sense in the material. The results should drive the choice of learning method, versus the learning methods driving the results. Accelerated learning is based on choosing the methods that work for a student to achieve their desired results.

So what type of results can drive the choosing of a learning method? Results might include the learning of a new and detailed skill set. Those in the skilled trades often use the learning method of encouraging their students to be hands on with both their tools and materials. As they practice together and under their instructor's watchful eye, they find themselves immersed completely in the material. The students are also benefitting from the experiences of their fellow students, thus contributing to a rich learning environment for everyone. It is easy to see how these skills can be mastered as students work diligently in a social and immersive environment.

This example leads to the importance of context in terms of learning. In the skilled trades, one has to understand how to use a tool in the proper context, building on their knowledge from tool to tool. Thus, their skill set continues to grow as one learning experience builds on another. Does this mean that facts by themselves are not important within the learning process? No, various pieces of data are necessary, even in a single fashion. Yet, accelerated learning focuses on creating context to the material. By doing so, the material is easier for the students to retain, because they understand how it relates to other aspects of the information. However, learning is a continual process. It involves immersing oneself in the material, then accepting feedback, reflecting and evaluating the results, then reimmersing one back into the education process. Accelerated learning promotes a complete immersion in the education process as critical to success.

Most students who have used this type of method to learn a new skill or a set of facts for a specific project or position find that they are able to retain more. Therefore, they are better able to execute their newly acquired skill set, as well as add to their knowledge through continual practice.

So what are a few of the techniques that can have learners helping themselves and each other? One such method is called the collaborative review circle. The class of students stands in a circle. Each student is provided a double-sided card with green on one side, but red on the other. When the students are questioned about a method or fact, those that believe they have the answer should flip their cards to green.

Those who do not know are meant to flip their cards to red. Those with the red card must find the answer by reaching out to one of the students who has a green card. Afterward, the instructor reveals the answer to the whole class. This method is geared toward the students helping each other. By assisting in teaching their fellow students, they are actually assisting in teaching themselves.

Instructors can also find that frequently stopping their presentations to engage their students in an activity can help them to process the information much faster. When a presentation builds using context learning as well, the results benefit from a combination of learning methods. Accelerated learning focused on the end game of acquiring a new skill or additional knowledge. One does not need to use every learning method, just the best combination for the student to truly immerse themselves into the learning process.

As we have seen, accelerated learning is about using a variety of methods, recognizing that the students will often dictate what works the best for them. Still there are some guidelines that must be mentioned when discussing accelerated learning. We will cover these guiding principles in the next chapter.

Chapter Two:
Accelerated Learning:
The Guidepost Principles

As with any learning method, certain guideposts provide the boundaries of how best to execute the method. While there might be several different ways to achieve the end results, accelerated learning relies on these guideposts to give instructors some guages when dealing with their students.

One of the first guideposts is that learning must involve the whole mind, as well as the body, to achieve the most long-lasting results. When we think of learning as merely involving the head, we shortchange ourselves both as teachers and students. In reality, we need to immerse ourselves with all of our senses, emotions and of course, the various information and data receptors available to our students. Learning a new skill might even involve taking time away from all other activities to give the immersion process our undivided attention. Yet, for many who follow this guidepost in their learning journey, they find it leads to much success and long term retention.

Another critical guidepost is the recognition of the building of a knowledge base as a creation on the part of the learner themselves. A student cannot consume knowledge but must build it as part of a larger learning process. When one is learning something, the student is putting in place new neural pathways, as well as integrating the information into the knowledge they already have. The result is the addition of new meanings, new patterns in terms of electro/chemical interactions and of course, new structures in how we think about the world based on newly acquired information. Thus, a student needs to feel empowered to build this knowledge base by means of their instructor, not stifled and thus unmotivated to create knowledge for themselves. This guidepost should cause the teacher to reflect on the importance of creating a positive and inviting learning environment right from the start.

Collaboration is another important guidepost of accelerated learning. Good learning methods are typically based on a social, collaborative platform. Our various interactions often contribute to the creation of our knowledge base. Students acquire so much information from their peers that it is critical to foster a sense of collaboration, instead of pitting students against each other in a competitive learning style. Isolated individuals will take longer to absorb information or new skills. For example, many colleges encourage students to build study groups. This method recognizes how important collaboration and cooperation are to the success of any student.

Learning often happens on multiple levels. This particular guidepost focuses on how information is acquired, not in a linear fashion, but essentially all at once. The brain is often processing multiple bits of information from the senses at the exact same time. Learning can and should occur in exactly the same fashion. Therefore, any teacher using the accelerated learning method should be focused on getting their students to learn through their conscious, sub-conscious, mental and physical states. Thus, the students is using all their body's receptors to gather the necessary information that will result in their building a large knowledge base. The brain can often be referred to as a parallel processor, so it thrives when challenged to compile and analyze information at a rapid rate from multiple platforms. A student who is learning on multiple levels can find it energizing, plus it contributes to long term retention on the brain's part.

For those who are learning a new skill, nothing is better than actually doing the work themselves. The brain can then be engaged on a multiple level platform. The five senses are completely in use as part of the learning process. When a student is provided feedback after completing a job or procedure, they are able to integrate and reflect on the feedback. Thus, adjustments can be made to the procedure or the work method to build on the student's knowledge base. Imagine working at a factory or another job that requires you to learn multiple processes at the same time. When trying to learn the task, repeating it frequently perhaps with instructions can really drive it into one's brain. Long term retention will be just one of the results, along with the satisfaction of having acquired a new skill.

Reimmersing oneself in a task after receiving feedback, which benefits from reflection. Students often find themselves better able to relate to information when presented in a concrete fashion, versus the use of abstract or hypothetical situations that might have little bearing on the current student's needs. As a student, one needs to look for real life applications of their new knowledge to keep it fresh but also to maintain their retention level.

Understand that another important guidepost is based on the emotional state of the student themselves. Stop for a minute and imagine a time when you have been particularly frustrated or angry. Did you try to pick up a new skill or add to your knowledge base during that time period? It probably did not end well. Can you even remember the skill you were attempting to learn? Most of us would reply with a negative to that question. On the other hand, when we have attempted to learn something while in a positive mood. The result is more affective knowledge building, plus there is better long term retention. Therefore, a student needs to approach their learning process with a positive attitude. Negative attitudes make it hard to grow and create a knowledge base. Learning in a dreary, stressful or painful fashion is not likely to last, but is more likely to be inhibited. When learning is based on a joyful, engaging and relaxing environment, the student is able to learn with both quality, as well as significant quantity.

Finally, one needs to remember that the brain does not function as a word processor. Instead, it is able to function as an image processor. Thus, the brain can consume large quantities of information via its entire nervous system. So do not sell your students short, just because there is a large amount of information to be absorbed. They can do it. To assist them, use concrete images versus verbal abstractions. If the information a teacher must impart is primarily verbal, then the teacher would need to translate the information into a variety of concrete images to assist their students in absorbing the necessary information.

As we have seen throughout our coverage of these guideposts, the most critical thing a teacher can do is listen to their students. What is working and what is not? Find out from the students and be willing to tweak your methods whenever necessary. Using these guideposts will help a teacher to create an environment that allows their students to freely build a knowledge base of both skills and data.

Still one needs to help their students keep mentally sharp. There are many methods for assisting someone to build their mental skills, sharpening both IQ and overall mental clarity. We will explore some of these methods and how as a bonus, they can provide memory enhancement as well.

Chapter Three:
Strategies to Expand the Mind's

Potential

As we have discussed throughout this book, learning is a whole body exercise, but that does not lessen the importance of the brain in the whole process. There are many students who feel limited by such things as their own IQ, or what they deem to be mental deficiencies. How can a teacher assist their student to overcome these perceived negatives to create a positive learning environment?

One of the best methods for doing so is by using environmental tools, such as music. There are researchers that have created at least four different strategies with music alone. Throughout this chapter, we will explore these four strategies and how to incorporate them into our learning techniques. The results can encourage a student and help them to create a positive learning environment to build their knowledge base.

Simply put, music can be used to enhance mood and memory. Thus, it can have an effect on how much a student absorbs, but also how much they are able to retain throughout the learning process. When listening to certain music, IQ and learning capability are enhanced, at least when the music is playing in the background. So what are the best musical pieces to use for mental enhancements? Classical pieces, including Mozart, Bach and Beethoven, have all demonstrated the ability to increase IQ as well as building an individual student's learning speed.

The University of California at Irvine has been the home of research on the effects of music on learning. The researchers found that those who listened to Mozart had an increase in their spatial IQ test by roughly nine points, while those who listened to a relaxation tape saw only a one point increase. Those subjects that did not listen to any music scored the lowest on the test. Researchers found that music did have a positive effect, but they also saw the effects did not last long after music ended. Still, by keeping this music as part of a student's learning process, a student can enhance their mental abilities with regular and more permanent long term results.

So how can one add music to their life on a regular basis? A student can do so by means of musical lessons. When musical lessons are part of a student's learning environment, they can often find themselves putting puzzles together faster than those who did not have musical lessons in their lives. Other research has shown that the benefits of music can best be captured with tasks that require the individual to create or engage in a task with mental imagery. When a task did not use mental imagery, the researchers found that music or even music lessons had little to no effect on the individual's ability to complete the task.

For young children, music lessons can provide benefits that last a lifetime. Their abilities when it comes to mental imagery can be extensive. Additionally, music has a relaxing effect on the brain, making it easier for a student to move into an active learning capacity. This ties into other research that found specific music and verbal inflections can be combined to create a natural and rhythmic memory aid as we shall see.

Out of that research came the Active and Passive Concerts. The Active Concert is best used with material that needs to be read. It combines verbal methods with relaxation and music. When building the Active Concert, one must read the information out loud in time with the music. Adding emotional flair helps to engrain the information even deeper into the brain of the student. The musical highs and lows provide a unique tempo for the reading. Additionally, the student is engaging their whole body by adding the rhythm to the reading. Then the ears and mouth get into the picture by both hearing and reading at the same time. Thus, the student is engaging with all of their senses. As we have learned, this promotes long term retention. Thus, music has a positive effect all the way around for a student.

Passive Concerts also follow the same tactics, but they use a softer voice and different musical backgrounds to create the effect. Researchers have found that these concert methods have long term effects on the memory and retention of new information. Beethoven is one composer that was found best for the Active Concerts, while Bach worked better with the Passive Concerts. Still, it is easy to see how engaging the brain on multiple levels using music can have some pretty amazing results for students.

Researchers have found that engaging with multiple senses, essentially information that we hear, see, say and do can result in a ninety percent retention rate. The percentages go down significantly if only one sense is involved in the learning process. Therefore, it is important to find ways to add multiple senses to any learning experience. Reading a chapter of a textbook for a particular class? Try reading the text out loud to music. By matching the words to the rhythm, one can create a memory aid while engaging at least two or more senses. Long term retention has been demonstrated to increase time and time again because one is able to engage with the information in a multilevel fashion.

Mental imagery is another method that researchers have found to be conducive to accelerated learning. As we learned in the early part of this chapter, music was affective in helping individuals learn mental imagery tasks, such as puzzles. But the use of mental imagery can be taken away from music and used on its own. Our imaginations provide us the ability to create pictures and imagery simply by reading the words on a page. Old time radio shows were designed to engage with their listeners' imaginations. Thus, the listeners provided the imagery themselves. There are some who believe that movies and television have reduced our brain's ability to create their own mental imagery or mental pictures. No matter where you fall on that argument, it is important to understand that mental imagery aids learning. So reading out loud, or pausing in your reading to build a mental scene, can help your imagination to flex its muscles. This will build your mental capabilities over the long haul and assist in your ability to retain larger chunks of information as part of the creation of a student's knowledge base.

Two specific memory options are also available to a student. One is to create a metaphor or an exaggerated story to match information one is trying to retain. For example, one can build a story around a list, using the words in the list as standouts within the story. Your brain can thus create a mental picture that will help you to remember the list in a long term fashion. When paired with an association technique, such as pairing the exaggerated story to music, a student can quickly find that they will remember the information within the story for a significantly long period of time.

After reading through the story along with the music, one should easily be able to recall the necessary information. But the important thing to remember that the story needs to have some pretty extensive exaggerations. After all, if the brain cannot build a wild mental image, this memory key will not be nearly as effective. However, it can be used with lists, chunks of information and even strategic plans.

Yet none of this is worthwhile if your student does not have a positive attitude toward the learning process. These techniques are not going to be as effective if they met with a negative attitude or scepticism. If your student is struggling, then it is important to encourage them by asking such questions as what do they gain from acquiring the information? A teacher can sometimes reach their student by simply appealing to their greed. After all, we all tend to work harder when we believe we will be benefiting in some way. Learning a new skill, for example, might result in a raise at our student's place of employment. But if they cannot learn the skill with a long term retention, it will do them little good. So you must help them to find that positive attitude. This goes back to the point of creating a positive and welcoming learning environment. So what is another method that students can use to reach that positive point of view? For many students, reflecting on periods of intense joy or success can bring them to a positive frame of mind. But how does one rebuild or recapture a feeling associated with an experience that happened years or even decades ago?

In the next chapter, we will discuss how the use of guided meditation can be effective in both memory enhancement, but also in creating a positive mental state for your students to flourish within. By following the method of guided meditation outlined, one can reach back into your past for some of the best feelings of your life and bring them forward to your learning experience in the present.

Chapter Four:
Using Guided Meditation to
Compliment Learning Techniques

Our brains and bodies are essentially one large camcorder. When we focus our concentration, we are essentially turning on the camcorder. Yet, whether we acknowledge it or not, our internal camcorder is constantly recording the sights and experiences of our world. How does the brain do this?

The brain relies on multiple organs throughout the body to gather the information it uses to create our sense of self and knowledge base. Overtime, the brain can often feel cluttered and make it hard to focus on any new information or skills. Thus, the brain uses various filing systems to essentially purge outdated information and replace it with more up to date facts. Experiences, especially those that received limited attention from us initially, are also often found in the memory's purge file. But for those who want to dig into the memories of their camcorder more intensely, they need a way to enhance their memory to achieve success. New students in the accelerated learning movement are also looking for methods that will help them to achieve a form of clarity, as well as mental enhancement in place of a cluttered camcorder brain and memory.

Meditation is a form of enhancement that can help one to create greater mental clarity. By focusing on moments when learning was successful, one can train the brain to repeat the event over and over again. Meditation assists in recreating these moments. Guided meditation allows for you to walk through specific steps to recreate a mental image of a specific moment in time or a distinct feeling during a period of achievement.

Below are a few of these guided meditations. Please keep in mind that one can create your own or use these. The idea is to tie movements of your body (the physical) with specific feelings and imagery (the mental), which means that you are providing your brain memory aids for digesting new data and other information or skills.

All meditation starts with breathing. It is important to take several slow deep breaths in and out before beginning any meditation. This will help you to relax prior to starting the more intense meditative sessions. While below is one meditation method meant to capture a feeling and associate with a specific physical movement, you can choose other memories and tie them to specific physical movements as well. Thus, this meditation can be adapted to a variety of settings.

Next, remind yourself of a particular experience where your student picked up a particular skill or data set easily. One example could be learning to ride a bike or another physical activity that was easy to pick up. Rebuild that scene of success into a mental image. Put yourself back into that place. Create the scene, include the various background imagery. Fix in your mind how you felt upon the success of that particular experience. Go back there in your mind. Reexperience the success, how it made you feel and how you achieved that success. Provide as much detail as possible, making a complete image and thus really immersing yourself into the experience.

Now capture your feeling of success and pinch your thumb and forefinger together. As the feeling passes, release your fingers. Continue to picture various moments of success. Each time you recreate the feeling of accomplishment, then pinch your thumb together with another of your fingers. Move through the index, middle, ring and finally the pinkie. Finally, pinch all the fingers together with the thumb. Associate this meeting of your fingers and your thumb with the feeling of success. Later, you can pinch your fingers together to remind yourself of that feeling. It can help to create a positive mental environment that is conducive to learning.

Other meditation methods rely on creating a memory aid by attaching a specific feeling or experience to a physical action. Thus, when the physical action is repeated, one can quickly and easily revisit to aid during any learning process. But ultimately, the student's ability to learn anything will be based on the teacher's creating the best possible environment for their students. During any accelerated learning course, an instructor needs to be actively engaging with their students to determine what is successful and what is not.

But how do your students reconnect with you after the accelerated learning course is completed? Followthrough is an important part of any learning course. This gives the instructor a chance to reconnect with their students and find out about their experience with the course. Have they been able to retain what was covered? Has it resulted in a better job performance or has the student been more successful at retaining critical information for specific tests?

The instructor can use follow-up forms to check up on their students. Another method is to add a follow up refresher course for your students. New students can be paired with previous students during the refresher course. This benefits the instructor, because they are able to gauge how well their students retained what they were taught. The students can also build on the social aspects of learning by teaching others, thus cementing it even further into their own brains.

Additionally, reminders geared to reinforce various points of the new skills or data should be used throughout the next few months after the training is completed. The idea is that by using reinforcement, one can keep your students engaged and building upon the original knowledge base they created in your course. However, these refresher options might not always be available. So a course might be geared to include graduates holding mini-training sessions of their own within their specific departments. This saves the company funds, while at the same time, it allows the students to reinforce what they have all been taught.

Accelerated learning relies on many different learning methods, but all of those methods are based on the idea that the student's best learning practices can be found within themselves. Companies in particular can use these accelerated teaching practices to spread new skill sets throughout various departments. How can one do this in a way that is cost effective? Simply put, one needs to keep in mind that training a few students and then allowing them to train others is an easy way to move skill sets through departments without the additional costs of training courses for all the employees.

One example would be to send all the department heads through an accelerated learning course. Then require the department heads to hold mini-sessions within their own departments. It is critical that the department heads employ the teaching methods used in their original course. Thus, these individuals in the position of management will be reinforcing what they have already learned, while saving the company's budget because they are now passing that knowledge on to the next crop of students.

Finally, as we have discussed with meditation, guide your students in various meditation techniques that they can pass on in their own training sessions. Overtime, the company will see the results of memory aids that the students can employ in multiple settings, both within their roles at the company, but also in other areas of their lives were memory retention and gaining new skills is critical.

Chapter Five:
The Importance of Memory to
Accelerated Learning

Throughout this book, memory had been mentioned more than once, and its importance to the learning process has been emphasized numerous times. Different descriptions of ways in which you can improve your memory have been explored, and if you followed these examples, you have probably managed to improve your memory to a certain extent. However, there have been very few examples to show you what memory is, and how important it is to the learning process. This chapter aims to clarify a few things about memory and the way it affects the learning process.

As you probably have deduced by now, there can be no learning without memory. Every organism on the planet that learns something has some form of memory, from the bee that has to learn how to get to a new food source, to the Rabbis who can recite the Torah word for word. However, to this day, there are still many schools of thought on memory and how it works. There are some things that we have found out though, and it is these things that you shall find out about in the following pages.

For instance, scientists have known for a while now that there are two basic types of memory: short term and long term memory. Each one is unique unto itself, yet they are both intricately linked and equally important to the learning process.

For example, if you were to do a simple math equation in your head, such as 19 x 7, the calculation would be carried out by your short term memory. If the answer you receive is important enough then the answer would be committed to your long term memory.

To use another example, all the sentences you have read in this book have been committed to your short term memory for a brief period. In most cases, it was probably just long enough for you to get to the end of the sentence so that you can make sense of the whole thing. Then, whatever information you (or your brain) thought that it needed was transferred to your long term memory.

When analyzing such examples, scientists discovered that your short term memory is more focused on analysis, while the long term memory is more concerned with synthesis. The same principles can be said to exist in a computer system, which is one reason why the brain is often compared to a computer.

Computers have two separate types of memory, RAM (Random Access Memory) and ROM (Read Only Memory). RAM is used mainly in processing, and the information on it is stored for a very short period of time, while ROM is used for more permanent storage. When you shut down a computer, all the information on the RAM is lost, but the information on the ROM survives which is almost the same thing that happens with the human brain. In this case, the RAM would be our short term memory, while the ROM would be our long term memory.

There are still many arguments on just how long short-term memory lasts, and numerous tests have been carried out. Despite the fact that the results for the tests are almost always speculative at best, the consensus is currently that it lasts for about 10 – 15 seconds. There have also been very many arguments as to HOW exactly the memories are stored,. However, it seems that short term memory is linked more to electrical impulses in the brain, while long term memory is linked to chemical processes, and the possible manipulation of proteins. So how can you change those electrical impulses into the proteins that serve as your long term memory, so as to enhance your learning abilities? (From this point onward, the term Memory will refer to the long term memory).

The Three 'R's of Memory

Memory may be difficult to understand, but there are things that we know for sure, because they have been tested and found to be true for hundreds of years. For example, the easiest way to remember something is to keep the three 'R's of memory in mind. these are Registration (encoding), Retention and Recall.

1. Registration – the awareness of the presence of new facts and the effort needed to commit these to long term memory.

2. Retention – the storage of these facts in long term memory

3. Recall – the ability to remember the facts when you need to.

One of the easiest ways to show just how different these steps are is to carry out a simple exercise. Below is a list of words lined up randomly in pairs. Read them through twice (That's the encoding part)

Play – Spy

Lamp – Place

Fox – Pen

Full – Book

Tree – Water

Far – Sink

Easy – Bike

Grass – Sand

Now, turn away from the page and try to remember as many words as you can, then look back at the list. If you can recognize all the words then you must remember them as well, meaning that you realize that you have seen them before. However, it is unlikely that you remember them correctly, or in the right order.

Recall is different from recognition. Recognition is the ability to partially recall something. For example, there are times when you have had something "on the tip of the tongue" but you just cannot say what it is aloud because you cannot remember it accurately enough. Should someone give you just the first syllable or two of the name, phrase or statement then completing it somehow becomes the easiest thing on the planet. You usually end up feeling like kicking yourself for not remembering. In scenarios like this, it is obvious that the first two of the three 'R's' have been successful, but the third has failed in one way or another.

This failure usually gets more pronounced as you get older. For instance, when the memory of senior citizens is tested, when they show signs of memory degradation it is not the first two steps that let them down but usually the third. Their recollection fails however, the ability to create and absorb information remains relatively intact.

Chapter Six:
Strategies to Affect Memory and Enhance Learning

It has already been made clear that one of the best ways to learn is to actually do or practice whatever it is you are trying to learn. This is because when you practice something, you are repeatedly registering the information, which helps to commit it to long term memory quicker. Numerous studies have shown that there is actually a direct correlation between the amount of practice that is carried out when learning something new, and the likelihood that the information will be remembered.

When considering practicing something, it is important to differentiate between practice, and repetition. Repetition alone cannot, and does not, improve your ability to learn, as repetition is just carrying out an exercise without involving yourself in it mentally. When you practice something, you are invested in it and therefore it registers itself in your memory quicker, and you can recall it more easily.

To demonstrate how different repetition and practice are, two psychologists carried out a test where they asked people to draw the features of one of the most commonly handled coins in the US. These people were guaranteed to have handled the coin thousands of times over a five year period, so you would think that reproducing the details on the coin would have been easy.

However, when the final results were tallied, nearly everyone who took part in the test had failed to recreate the detail on the coin. This was attributed to the fact that while they handled the coin multiple times a year, it was a repetitive action, and the people were not invested in taking in the details of the coin.

Two British psychologists from Cambridge observed the same result when the BBC in was changing its wavelengths. The BBC had been running an ad campaign to announce the change in frequencies for a few months, meaning that the group of people tested should have heard the advert at least a hundred times by the time the study was being carried out. However, when asked to reproduce certain details in the advertisement, once again most people failed, with many of them literally resorting to guess work to try and fill in the details.

There are many other ways you can improve the learning process other than practice. For instance, there are certain things that you will not even have to memorize to learn. Certain sequences and patterns can be recalled accurately as long as the principle involved is understood. For instance, mathematical sequences such as the Fibonacci sequence do not have to be learned if you understand the principle behind them.

Many studies have revealed that when trying to learn something, it is much more effective if you remember the principle behind what you are trying to learn, rather than the specifics. When it comes to accelerated learning, it is therefore much easier to remember the principle rather than the actual information. This is one of the easiest ways for you to amass a large amount of information in the memory with the least amount of effort. It is also easier to trigger a recall of information if you remember the principle behind it.

For instance, the English speakers in an Accelerated Learning German class found it very hard to differentiate the different genders for words in the foreign language. However, after being given a mnemonic exercise that emphasized the principles behind the association of genders, they were able to deduce the different genders of words based on those principles. This ability to deduce the genders of different words in seconds meant that they were able to learn German at an increased pace.

Another way to help you remember, and therefore increase the chance that you will learn something quickly is to attach meaning to that thing. In 1975, researchers Craik and Tulving carried out a study to find out how people would remember a set of 60 words. The criteria they used were the visual appearance of the words, the sound of the words, or the meanings of the words.

They found that when it comes to the appearance and sound of the words, people would recall less than 30% of the words presented to them. However, when asked about the meaning of the words, people would recall almost 75% of all the words that they were asked to remember.

In its simplest form, this study showed that unless you attach some sort of meaning to something, and you understand it, then your ability to learn about that thing will drop drastically. Once you have attached meaning to it, then your brain will be able to associate it with other things or pieces of information, making it easier for you to remember. Therefore, if you are not involved in absorbing the information, it will not be processed properly and it will literally 'go in one ear and out the other'.

This also explains why practice and repetition are so important to learning. By practicing and repeating exercises and information, you are attaching meaning to those things, making them easier to recall in the future.

Chapter Seven:
How Sleep Affects Memory

One of the most effective ways to learn something is to sleep. This may seem counterintuitive, as most people assume that to learn something you have to be awake. However, there are studies that show that a good night's sleep may actually be one of the most effective ways for you to learn how to do something.

If you were to think of the brain as a computer, then it may be easier for you to understand this concept. Think of the times when a computer needs to go 'offline' to be upgraded or reprogrammed. It is usually during this time that the new programs are tested and the old programs modified to be able to perform any new tasks. The same can be said about the human brain.

When we sleep, we are essentially putting the conscious mind in an 'offline' state. This is usually when the subconscious comes online, and begins to run through all the events of the day, committing them to memory, and integrating them into new patterns of behavior, thought and belief. This is usually done during REM (Rapid Eye Movement) sleep, which is incidentally the time when we dream.

REM sleep accounts for about 25% of the total sleep cycle in adults. It happens about four times every night, and is when sleep becomes most paradoxical. This is because as much as the conscious brain is asleep, this is when the brain becomes most active, and when connected to an ECG machine, it shows a spike in activity. This activity could be attributed to dreams, or it could be attributed to the subconscious processing the information that the brain has absorbed during the day.

There have been a number of studies to show that this is when the subconscious reprograms the brain, at least marginally anyway, and those studies go as far back as 1968. This was when researchers concluded that there were parts of dreams that were related to the unconscious processing of information. They also found that the more information one absorbs during the day, the more REM sleep the brain will undergo, and therefore the more a person will dream.

Numerous researchers have also stated that it seems that dreams act as rehearsals for the things that we expect to happen. For instance, if you dream that you are speaking a foreign language, and you happen to be learning that language at the same time, it may be your brain's way of reinforcing the lessons that you received during that day.

When it comes to learning, many mothers agree that when their children first start going to school, they seem more willing to sleep than usual. This has been attributed to the fact that the body knows that to be able to absorb all the information that they have received during the day, they need to undergo REM sleep to help retain the knowledge that they have gained and therefore recall it more easily in the future.

Taking a break from learning or studying is almost as important as getting a good night's sleep, and can drastically improve your chances of recalling information accurately. It has been found that taking a 5 minute break every half hour can increase your chances of recalling information that you have absorbed significantly.

Earlier in this book, we discussed how the different learning environments could affect accelerated learning. However, that was mainly when considering the mental and emotional aspects of the environment. Many studies have shown that the actual physical environment is also important to learning, and that it actually can directly affect how we remember different things.

For instance, when American astronauts are training for missions on the International Space Station, one of the main ways they are prepared for the rigors of living and working in space is by training 40 feet underwater in a special tank. The environment in the tank simulates everything that they are going to have to get used to while they are in space, including how to get around in zero gravity, and how to use their equipment in such conditions.

By doing this, certain movements and protocols become committed to memory so that when they finally do get to the space station, they are better prepared and able to learn quicker.

Learning how to work in a certain environment can be accelerated by learning in simulated environments, but the environment itself can also be very important in the way that we remember things. In keeping with the underwater theme, there was a study carried out where a number of scuba divers were placed into two groups, and taught the same set of words. One group was taught the words while they were underwater, while the other was taught the on the shore. When the divers were tested, it was found that those who learned the words underwater and were tested underwater were twice as likely to remember all they were taught, compared to those that were taught on the shore but tested underwater.

In a completely different experiment, there was a man who was taught how to dance in a room with a chest in the middle of it. While he was in the room, he was one of the best dancers the researchers had ever encountered, and his grace and poise were impressive. However, when he was taken out of the room, or if the chest was removed, he would struggle with the simplest of steps, and became clumsy and ungainly. When he was placed in a foreign room with a chest in it, his dancing improved, and he was back to his graceful ways.

These two tests served to show that there people recall what they have learned better when they are in the same environment they learned it in. Therefore, when learning anything, real world experience is better than simulations. It was also found that people learn better in the same setting, even if the setting is as tiny as a desk in an office. One finding that may seem strange was that when recalling information, many people tend to recall the environment in which they learned that material as well, not just the information itself.

Chapter Eight:
Additional Memory Aids

Throughout this book, you have read about many different ways to help you remember information. In this section, we shall look at some of the more overlooked strategies that can be used to help you learn faster, and how you can use them to your advantage.

One of the most influential papers in the history of psychology, "The Magical Number Seven, Plus or Minus Two: Some Limits on Our Capacity for Processing Information", was published in 1956 in the Psychological Review. Its author, renowned psychologist George A. Miller, suggested that the human memory span was limited to the number of items that it can hold.

His research found that when given a list, whether it was of words or numbers, people could never correctly remember the items on the list if it had more than about seven items on it, hence 7 plus or minus 2. As you discovered earlier, short term memory lasts for about 10 seconds, and in that time, it is usually unlikely for anyone to be able to sub-vocalize more than 7 items therefore committing them to long memory.

However, Miller was quick to point out that it was the number of items that limited the brain, not the information that those items held. For instance, tt is obvious that if there were only one word attached to each item on the list, then it would be easy to remember more than seven items. However, should there be a wealth of information per item, or a chunk of information as Miller called it, then you could increase the amount of information stored in the list, and therefore remember more information.

This process of putting things in little packages or chunks is actually a very natural process, and follows a specific pattern. For example, try to commit the following series of numbers to memory: 4 8 5 9 2 6 1 7 1 2. While you were reading the numbers, you would probably committed them using the format 485-926-1712. This 'chunking' up of the numbers is a natural process, and is something that is evident all over the globe.

An even more obvious example of chunking is the way we recite the alphabet. There are 26 letters in the alphabet, but when we recite them we do not go through them as one whole stream, but as chunks of seven syllables. To make it even easier, we associate a rhyming rhythm to the recitation, which helps us remember the alphabet even quicker. In fact, even when we are asked to give a letter that is either before or after another, for instance, if you are asked to name the letter before P, the likelihood that you will begin to recite the alphabet from H is pretty high, as that is where the rhythm begins for that particular phrase.

Rhythm and Rhyme and Visualization

Rhythm and Rhyme are another reason why monks chant their prayers. Almost every religion on the planet chants their prayers, be they Muslim, Christian, Buddhist, or Hindi, the mnemonic advantages of rhythm and rhyme are exploited to help the faithful remember their prayers.

Rhythm and rhyme are one reason why music is so effective when it comes to aiding accelerated learning. Many people do not even realize this, but there are times when the subconscious begins to assign the rhythm of the piece that is being heard to the words that are being read or the information that is being absorbed. This helps the brain encode and recall the information easier.

This is also the main reason why parents around the globe become frustrated with their teenage children when they can remember the words to a pop song with minimal exposure, yet they cannot remember the math questions they solved in class a few hours before.

Another reason why children may remember the words to a pop song more than their math problems is the fact that teenagers will usually be motivated to remember the words of their favorite song more than they will be to remember a math problem. The question of motivation has been approached before in this book, and this is the perfect example to illustrate that.

They become motivated to learn the song because it is fun, stress free, and seems more rewarding to them. This is in much the same way that young children learn in pre-school and kindergarten. The lessons are made as fun as possible, and because the children enjoy their lessons so much, they excel at them. This creates a cycle of learn/enjoy/succeed that usually fuels more interest in the subject, encouraging the individual to go back to the beginning and go through the whole thing again.

Many people use this principle when practicing Accelerated learning. In many accelerated learning courses, the information is made as fun as possible for the students, which helps to motivate them to learn. When they realize that their enthusiasm yields results, it only motivates them to learn even more, and in a short period of time the information, they find that they have absorbed a lot of information.

The same is true for children when they are learning how to speak, except that with them, they are using the principles that we use consciously unconsciously. The learn how to communicate alarmingly quickly partly due to the fact that they find it fun, but also because it is the only way that they can get what they want, and that motivates them to learn.

There are very many ways you can motivate yourself to learn something new. One of the simplest ways to do so is to set yourself goals, then when you have achieved those goals, treat yourself to something. It could be a new jacket, a new pair of shoes, dinner and a movie, or even just an extra hour in bed. Whatever the case may be, the reward should be enough to help you learn whatever you have set out to learn quicker.

One way that is better than rhythm and rhyme when it comes to aiding memory is visualization. There is a reason there is a saying that goes "A picture is worth a thousand words", and that is because to the brain, this really is true.

To demonstrate this, there was a study carried out in 1970 at the University of Rochester New York, where participants were shown 2,500 photographs over seven hours. When the session was over, they were shown another series of 600 photographs. In the second series of photographs were photos from the first series in random order as well as a few new images. The participants of the experiment were supposed to identify the pictures that they had seen before, and by the end of the exam, all had recognized at least 98% of the photos.

A second test group was shown the same 2,500 pictures, except in their case, after the initial viewing, they were shown a series of 300 pairs of photographs over 3 days. In their case, they were able to recall at least 85% of the photographs correctly. The experiment proved just how important images are to the mind, and how easy it is for the brain to remember pictures.

Combining Rhythm, Rhyme and Visualization

These two concepts can be taken a step further to help you remember a list of unrelated items in the right order. When combined, rhythm and rhyme, and visualization allow you to create what are known as peg words.

To create peg words you first have to think of objects that rhyme with numbers, and then commit them to memory. A good example is the list below.

One = Fun

Two = Through

Three = Glee

Four = More

Five = Jive

Six = Picks

Seven = Shaven

Eight = Fate

Nine = Dine

Ten = Pen

Once you have memorized the words, you can begin to visually relate the items that you need to remember with the peg words.

For instance, if you are supposed to remember a list of things that your child would like for Christmas, and the third item is a toy boat, you would need to get the boat and the tree to interact in the most memorable way possible. You may choose to picture a boat hanging precariously off the top branch of a tall tree that is the middle of a forest, or you may decide to picture a fruit tree that grows miniature boats instead of fruit.

The fifth item on the list may be an alarm clock. In this case, you could decide to visualize a hive of clocks instead of bees, and instead of hearing the buzz of bees as you approach the hive, all you hear is the ringing of the alarm. This is one of the best ways to use peg words, as you engage more than one sense in the visualization, increasing the chances of it sticking in your memory.

Mnemonic experts suggest that when you are visualizing such scenarios, you make them as vivid, unusual, and funny as you possibly can to help you retain the information. The fact that these images are all in your head and will not be seen by anyone means that you can make them as vulgar as you want, and a number of experts actually agree that the more vulgar and sexual the image the better, as they will engage the most senses.

Chapter Nine:
The Lozanov Method of
Accelerated Learning

The first true practitioner of accelerated learning as we know it today was a Bulgarian research psychologist called Dr. Georgi Lozanov. He introduced a whole new way of teaching, and today an evolved form of his method of teaching is used in schools around the world, from Europe to North America. The method of teaching may have changed, but the principles that he used remain the same, and are successful regardless of the culture that they are translated to.

For instance, there is a group of UNESCO (United Nations Education and Scientific Cultural Organization) officials that was that were taken to a class and informed that in two short lessons, they would have learned and be able to recall at least 1,200 new words in a foreign language, in their case Spanish. Obviously, they were did not believe what they were hearing, but to please the teacher, they decided to sit through the class anyway.

The class would follow the Lozanov method of teaching and would therefore follow his six key steps. However, before the six steps had even been initiated, the class had already begun. The classroom was filled with posters and pictures of familiar objects and animals labeled in Spanish, as well as a music system that was playing music. The seats in the class were arranged in a semi-circle to create a more informal, relaxed setting, rather than having the proper desks and chairs that would be associated with a classroom.

The first step is de-suggestion. In this case, the teacher had to remove the idea from the officials' brain that they are limited, and that they cannot learn more than a finite amount of information at a certain speed. This is because it is exactly these self inflicted restrictions that lead to the brain limiting ITSELF to a certain way of learning.

These restrictions are placed in our minds early in our development by both culture and the school systems that we follow. The restrictions are then replaced by the implication that learning is simple, fun, and enjoyable. Basically, this step takes our brains back to the way they used to be before about five years old, when the whole world was fascinating and there was an infinite amount of knowledge to be absorbed.

The second step is centered on relaxation, and is important because to learn anything quickly, one has to be completely stress free. This step is where the teacher creates the learning environment that was discussed earlier, and ensures that their students are comfortable and ready to receive information.

The third step involves mapping out the information that the students are going to learn, so as to introduce them to the material that they are going to absorb. This allows them to familiarize themselves with the material, and prepares them for what they should expect. In the case of the UNESCO officials, the class was presented to them in English first, so that they could understand what they would be expected to know at the end of the lesson. The second part of the mapping process involved going through the whole lesson again in Spanish so that they could get a feel of it.

The fourth step was the Active concert. The lesson was read to some Baroque music (music composed between 1700 and 1750), in a dramatic manner, and in time with the music. The officials were asked to read the book while following the sound of the language. The text in the books they were given was laid out in such a way that the Spanish was in the center of the page, but the English translations were on the periphery. This made sure that though the conscious brain was not focused on the translations, the subconscious mind (that internalized everything) was able to internalize the translations as well.

This step includes some very important subliminal elements. The music acts as a direct route to the subconscious by triggering different emotions through harmony, rhythm and thyme. This creates a shortcut to the brain that logical facts and arguments cannot follow. It also stimulates both sides of the brain simultaneously and independently, increasing the pace at which the information is absorbed into the memory.

The fifth step is usually preceded by a short break, after which the Receptive or Passive concert begins. This was one of the more baffling steps for the UNESCO officials, as for them it seemed like it required no effort on their part. They were told to sit back in their chairs, close their eyes and relax, and just listen to the music. In this step, the music is the dominant factor in the class, while the Spanish lesson (repeated in a softer tone by the teacher) becomes the background sound.

 Though they thought this was pointless, what they did not know at the time was that this step is crucial, as it further engages the subconscious and sidesteps the conscious mind almost completely. In the case of a language class, the receptive concert helps your brain to learn and understand the intonations, patterns and rhythms that are used when speaking the language.

When the teacher completed reading the Spanish to them again, the class was dismissed. It had lasted two hours. The teacher explained that the first lesson was meant to initiate the coordination of the left and right hemispheres of the brain so as to increase their learning capacity. By using this method, the learning capacity of most people can increase drastically, from three times as much to ten times as much.

The next day, after everyone had had a good night's sleep, the last and final step in the learning process could begin.

The class began with what the teacher called activations, and the officials were introduced to a number of games and puzzles that had been specially designed to help them go through the words that they had learned in the first class. The games were designed to be deliberately childlike so that they could be as fun as possible. One reason for this is that Lozanov maintained that the most crucial part of this exercise was to regress to the way children learn BEFORE they go to school. In this way, even if you fail at something, the stress that is usually associated with failure cannot arise. Additionally, learning like that is characterized by an expectation of success, meaning that any mistakes made are looked at as a sign that the student has overstretched themselves, which is a sign of ambition and shows an absence of fear.

Of the various games, the one that received a unanimous vote from the officials was one that involved a ball. In this game, the teacher would throw a ball to a student while simultaneously asking a question in Spanish. The student would answer as they caught the ball, which surprised many, as they did not think that they would know the answer, especially without having to think about it.

The answers came easily because the ball was used to distract the conscious mind, leaving the unconscious to reply to the question. The officials had absorbed the information from the previous day's class while they were asleep, and this review the next day was helping to cement the information in their long term memory.

There are many things that contributed to the subconscious gaining this information other than the music and the Active and Receptive concerts. The textbooks had vivid pictures that helped to stimulate the subconscious and create suggestions in the subconscious mind. The outline of these pictures usually had the word for the object or animal it was representing written in Spanish in the outline. For instance, the outline of a lion had the word 'leon' written into it.

In addition, the officials were all given Spanish names and characters at the beginning of the class. This was so that they would feel that if they got anything wrong, it was not necessarily their fault, but the fault of their Spanish 'alter ego'. The class became a role play session as well, increasing the 'fun' aspect of it, and therefore creating an even more conducive learning environment.

This method is so successful when it comes to teaching languages, that students have been reported to learn languages fluently in as little as a month. Many of these students were able to recall 90% of the words they learned every day, and the words themselves would usually number in the hundreds.

Something that is revealed to all those who have practiced this method of learning is this; play is central to learning. It is one of the only ways we can act out the different ideas that we need to learn. In fact, there are some psychologists that say that play is the daytime version of dreaming because of just how important it can be to learning.

Chapter Ten:
The Importance of Music to
Accelerated Learning

As was mentioned earlier, music is very important when used to aid in learning, and can be used to accelerate the learning process considerably. In this chapter, we shall take a more in depth look at how music can shape accelerated learning.

The fact that music can affect the way people learn things is something that has been known for the longest time. For example, the Ancient Greeks would hold a festival every four years where people would go to the Panathenes every four years and listen to the Iliad presented to the rhythm of a heartbeat and a lyre. This was done from memory, which is a feat unto itself. Records reveal that at the end of the show, many of the people who had come to watch the presentation could remember large passages afterwards. This has been attributed to the music that was played during the show, as it helped the attendees to remember the show.

The philosophers Plato and Aristotle also discussed the way music helps to harmonize the soul and body. In fact, Plato went a step further and said that "The character of a nation's music cannot be altered without changing the customs and institutions of the State". This is a very powerful statement, and shows just how important Plato thought music was to civilization.

There is evidence of monks in the ancient world using music to help them study. Some of these monks are famous around the world to this day as some were able to memorize whole books without an issue.

Music has also been used to change the moods of people so that they can learn faster. For instance, the mystics of India have used music for centuries to help them achieve a heightened meditative state, and to control pain. The musicians of North Africa used to believe that music had a magical quality to it because of the influence it had on people's emotions. Bach was so good at manipulating human emotion with his music that he composed the Goldberg Variations for the Russian envoy Count Kayserling to help him sleep.

Music is so powerful when it comes to affecting human emotions, that researchers have found that some of the goals that people strive towards with weeks of meditation can actually be realized in minutes with the right kind of music. This is usually thanks to the rhythm of the music, and the different tones that it is composed of.

Rhythm is at the center of everything that around us. There is rhythm in everything, from the tiniest atom to the largest celestial body in the universe. Humans are governed by rhythm, and half the time we do not even realize it. Our daily routines are very rhythmic, and even our bodily functions follow a certain rhythm.

The fact that rhythm affects everything has been tested numerous times using music as a source for the rhythm. For instance, studies carried out on plants have found that plants that have music played to them will have (on average) 70% more leaves and grow 20% taller if they have music played to them. Studies carried out in Canada's Ottawa University found that different plants react differently to different types of music. They found that music can increase seed production and increase chances of germination in different plants, and that these plants will actually show a preference for the types of music that they enjoy by accelerating their growth depending on the frequencies they are exposed to.

A separate, comparative study was carried out at the University of Denver by a Mrs Rettallack in 1977. The study found that plants responded more positively to classical music, especially Bach, and select classical Indian sitar music, than they did to Rock music. In fact, most of the flowers tested died after two weeks of listening to rock music.

No one knows for sure why plants and other living organisms react in such a positive way to baroque music, but the fact that it resonates so well with all living organisms including humans is something that cannot be denied. In fact, some researchers believe that baroque musicians, in an attempt to create the perfect mathematical form in their music, managed to create work that produces the right frequencies and sounds to create a calm, relaxed and yet alert mind. This state is the reason why baroque music is so central to the Lozanov technique described in the previous chapter.

The Effect of Music on Brain Waves

There are other forms of music that resonate on this level, with the most obvious being classical Indian music. Classical Indian music was composed to help create specific meditative states, and therefore it also creates a calm, relaxed yet alert state in the body. This state, whether produced by Baroque music or Classical Indian music, tends to increase a person's capacity to absorb information.

To prove this, Stephen Cooter, and educational theorist, examined his brain waves on an ECG (electrocardiogram) during two different scenarios, when he was in an ordinary waking state, and while he was listening to Baroque music that had been recommended for the active concert part of Lozanov's accelerated learning course.

He found that when in an ordinary waking state, his Beta waves (the waves that keep you critically alert) dominated the scale, while the Alpha waves (that help with relaxation and meditation) were the next on the list. His Theta waves (that helped to induce sleep) were the most inactive types of waves.

However, when listening to Baroque music, especially when he listened to the whole composition, he ended up with a balanced brain wave composition. He noted that the largo movements in these pieces would induce more Theta waves, but when the composition was listened to as a whole, the brain waves balanced themselves out.

This is important when it comes to accelerated learning, especially when using the Lozanov method. Because of these findings, instructors of this method started using whole compositions during their classes, rather than just exerts, because they helped to provide the full daily emotional cycle in a short amount of time.

To test just how effective the music was to learning, researchers from the University of Texas split a class into 3 groups. Each group was given a list of vocabulary that they were supposed to study and given different ways in which to study the list.

The first group had the list of words recited to them, with Handel's Water music playing in the background. In addition, they were asked to visualize the words as they were read out to them. The second group had the same list read to them, with the same music playing in the background, except the instruction to visualize the words was omitted. The third group just had the words read to them.

When they were tested at the end of the experiment, it was found that the first two groups had a marked improvement in performance over the third group, with the first group faring the best overall. When they were tested a week later, the first group were still the best group of them all, except now the gulf was much bigger between them and the second group.

This led the researchers to conclude that the results proved that the multiple senses that were engaged when learning the vocabulary, coupled with the participation of both hemispheres of the brain, allowed for learning to occur at a quicker pace.

Chapter Eleven:
Children and Accelerated Learning

There is currently debate about whether accelerated learning techniques are suitable for young children, especially those in pre-school to elementary school. However, the one thing that almost everyone agrees on is that children need to learn in a rich environment to realize their full potential.

When it comes to older children, the most important thing that teachers and parents can remember is that the brain is like a muscle, the more you work on it, the better it will perform. Glenn Doman said it best when he said "The brain has infinite capacity. The more you put in it, the more it will hold."

He argued that the best way to teach a child is for the parent to teach the child at normal speeds, and not slow anything down because "they are too young". He said that by doing this, you imply to the child that they cannot learn fast enough, and therefore their brains automatically slow down the learning process so that they can keep up with you and your low expectations of them. This process inevitably leads to the child losing their latent ability to learn.

In short, if you expect a lot from your child, they will achieve a lot. A child's ability to register, retain and recall information is much higher than that of an adult which is why they can learn so much at a young age. It is also why the Lozanov method uses elements that try to recreate the way a child takes in information.

When considering accelerated learning for children, people usually ask very many questions, such as:

- Are women the best teachers?

- Does positivity affect children the same way it affects adults?

- How should we (as parents/teachers) answer the questions that children ask?

The answers to these questions surprise some, because the answers though obvious are not things that people really think about.

The answer to the first question is yes, women, especially mothers, seem to be the best teachers. This is because, without any formal training, they manage to supervise what has been termed the most important, yet dramatic period of learning in every human life. They are the ones who teach their children the most important life lessons in their earliest years, from how to walk to how to communicate.

They are the ones that begin to instill morals in their children, and they are responsible for the way the child sees the world in those first years. They instinctively create a positive learning environment for a child, and cultivate the emotional responses that children have to learning. Mothers also help to encourage their children, praising them when they succeed, and correcting them when they get something wrong by showing them how to do it right. They very rarely focus on the error that was made, therefore encouraging the child to make mistakes and learn from them. Perhaps the most important thing mothers give their children is the ability to visualize through the stories that they tell.

Various observational studies have concluded that children from families where the thinking of the child is respected, their creativity is encouraged, and where human and intellectual values are prized, inevitably succeed in life when they grow older. However, in families where the child is berated, chastised, and condemned as foolish, patterns of failure develop that inevitably lead to the wastage of a great mind.

An example of just how damaging negative reinforcement can be to a child, a famous Lawyer, David Dow, used the example of death row inmates in Texas. He posited that almost all the inmates on death row in Texas correctional facilities had basically the same life story. They came from broken homes, normally with one or two abusive parents, and they were never encouraged in any way to better themselves or to learn from their mistakes. This in turn led them to learn down the wrong path in life as failure was expected of them, and it was only once they ended up facing the hangman's noose that some of them realized that they could have made different choices in life. Though this may be an extreme example, it goes to show how important it can be to be positive when teaching your children.

Effects of Positivity and Encouragement

In fact, when it comes to a child's education, especially if you would like to increase their learning capacity, good music and books, art and pictures, and creating a sense of fun and adventure towards learning are only half the fight. The other half of the battle involves being positive and encouraging questions.

Positivity is needed not only because it encourages your child and helps them succeed in the future, but also because it encourages the absorption of information, and therefore encourages learning. One of the most important things you can do for a child is show them that learning can be easy, and that they can attain the results that they are looking for even if they fail once or twice on their way to the final result.

However, this does not mean that you should pay no attention to the reality of the situation. It just means that one bad grade on a test is just that, one bad grade. It does not mean that your child is 'no good' at whatever it is they are learning, it just means that the information that they were given was not absorbed properly.

The actual mistake is not the most important thing, what is important is that the child will succeed if encouraged to cultivate their creativity. One of the easiest ways to cultivate creativity is to encourage questions. Children are naturally inquisitive, and can have an endless supply of questions to ask you as they grow. This is out of a curiosity that is instinctive, and in the past, this curiosity is what helped the human race to survive. For prehistoric humans, asking questions about their environment such as what foods could be eaten or what animals could be approached would ensure that a child would survive to reproduce and maintain the survival of the species. Today, despite the fact that that part of learning to survive is not that important, the instinctive curiosity is still there, and the desire to learn everything about the world is something that children, especially young children, still have.

Encouraging them to ask questions increases their ability to learn, after all, as stated before, the more information you feed the brain, the more it can absorb. However, the way you answer those questions is important if you want to encourage learning. If you answer a question that provides finality, then you will not encourage the child to think any further. However, if you leave your child with something to think about and reflect upon, you will find that you can stoke their curiosity, which will encourage them to ask even more questions.

Chapter Twelve:
Teaching your child using Accelerated Learning Techniques

If you do decide to try and teach your child using some accelerated learning techniques, it is important that you follow some guidelines and keep some things in mind.

For starters, just like with the Lozanov method, you must create a map or outline of the main points of the lesson. You can use a list of key words and phrases to help out outline the ideas that you would like your child to learn. The words should then be written down so that they can be used later during your lesson with the child, to help elaborate what you are trying to communicate to them. These words should be hung up around the room that you are going to use so that they can serve as a constant reminder to what the lesson is about. Even if your child does not consciously absorb them, their unconscious will surely take note and integrate them into memory.

If the words can be accompanied by vivid pictures this would be even more effective. Just as with visualizations, the more vivid, bizarre, funny or dramatic, the better, as these will be absorbed faster. Remember, the principles of any subject you are trying to teach are actually more important than the information. You also have to remember to try as much as possible to present the information in "chunks" rather than continuously so that they are retained better.

Creating an Active and Passive concert for each lesson would also be beneficial to the child. Keep in mind that the rhythm of your words should go with the rhythm of the music as much as possible, as should the intonations of your words and the volume with which you speak. When rehearsing, (you will realize that these concerts are basically performances, so you need to rehearse), try to raise and lower your voice in time with the different movements and inflections in the music. Try to act out the lesson as well, exaggerating certain movements to emphasize a point. Remember to keep it fun and unexpected to keep the child engaged, as this will help them retain and recall the information quicker. If you can, record the different concerts so that your child can play them back at their own leisure.

Finally, remember to keep the games that you play during the activations as interactive and fun as possible. Be as creative as you can with the games, and try to use games that your children can already identify with to help them learn quicker. For instance, if you are trying to teach them a language, card games are very effective when it comes to learning numbers. You can play "simon says" to help teach verbs, and "I Spy" to help reinforce the names of different items and objects.

Using TV game shows can also help you teach them adjectives and sentence structures, as can games like charades which are so engrossing that the child may actually get lost in their own world while speaking the new language. One of the best ways to teach older children the nuances of language is to get them to watch shows and news bulletins in the foreign language, and then make a game out of deciphering the nuances of what is being said on screen.

It is also important to remember that the same things that apply to adults when practicing accelerated learning apply to the children as well. For instance, it is important that your children are relaxed before you begin the class, as this will accelerate the absorption of information. If the music does not work to this end in the beginning, try a few relaxation exercises together.

It is also important to remember that these lessons are supposed to be enjoyable, therefore if you or your children are not having fun, and find interest waning, stop and try again the next day. Also, keep in mind that these lessons are supposed to be short. For children, anything more than about 90 minutes is too much, however, less than 45 minutes is too short, so try and keep your lessons between that time frame.

You should also understand that some children will be resistant to this method of learning at first, especially if they are successful in their formal education. This is because they have already gotten so used to the adage that effort = results, and they are already getting certain rewards from their classical education. It will be hard for them to see the rewards that they are getting from the accelerated learning practices that you are showing them, mostly because they will think it is too easy.

This is usually just their subconscious talking, and usually, the subconscious tries to prove itself right. In most cases though, the child will realize that their subconscious is wrong when they begin to see just how much information they can recall after such a short time, and they will begin to open up to the idea of accelerated learning.

The active and passive concerts that you recorded for your child should be stored somewhere where they can access them whenever they want. These days, that's usually on their smartphones or tablet, so make sure that they have those recordings on those items at all times. Also, keeping in mind how the brain stores information, you should encourage your children to play the passive concerts in the late evening or at night and the active concert the following morning. This will allow the subconscious to assimilate the information from the passive concert during REM sleep, while the active concert in the morning will act as a conscious review of the information, helping to reinforce it. This method is very effective, especially with children who are going to be tested that day.

Lastly, keep in mind that people learn best in groups, and the same goes for children. If you can get your child to form a group with friends and neighbors, even if it is just a small group of four or five people, it will be that much easier for your child to learn quickly. In addition, you will not only be helping your child, you will also be helping someone else's child. You will also be helping yourself, by learning what methods work and which methods you should discard, which will help you be a better teacher to your children.

Chapter Thirteen:
Frequently Asked Questions About
Accelerated Learning

In this chapter, we shall look at some of the questions that people ask about accelerated learning, and try to clarify some of the things that many people find confusing.

1. Does our current educational system really stifle our ability to learn quickly?

The simple answer to this is YES, it does. Glenn Doman carried out a study on a number of children that ran over the course of three years. At the beginning of the study, he held up a number of cue cards with dots on them, and asked the children to count the dots. They could all accurately give the number of dots on the cards without even counting. This was attributed to the fact that they were able to visualize the cards easily, and therefore did not need to count in a linear manner.

However, three years later, when the same children were presented with the same cards, they took their time to answer the question because now they were counting in a linear fashion. By training the children to count in this way, the teachers had inadvertently stifled the children's ability to visualize the dots and therefore they could not give an answer instantaneously. This is just one of the many examples that is used to show how classical education can restrict the brain's ability to function at its full potential.

2. How does Peripheral Learning Work?

The easiest way to understand how peripheral learning works is to use the example of a study that Dr. Lozanov conducted years ago.

He got a group of 500 students to memorize a list of 10 towns. Of these 10 towns, five had been underlined in color, but the color was so faint it was barely perceptible. They were then presented with a list of 180 towns and asked to select the original 10 towns that they were shown. After this exercise, they were asked to identify which of the ten towns had been underlined, and in what color.

The test was then repeated over an additional 59 days. The students were never shown the original 10 towns again, but by the end of the 60 days, the towns that were remembered the most from the list were the towns that had been imperceptibly underlined.

The inevitable conclusion was that peripheral learning is very effective.

3. Does Peripheral Learning stop working when you know about it?

No, it does not. If anything, the fact that your brain knows it exists INCREASES its effectiveness by almost 10%.

4. Does Accelerated Learning use Subliminal Techniques?

No, it does not. There is a very big difference between peripheral and subliminal communication.

Peripheral communication is designed in such a way that if you wanted, you could bring whatever is in your periphery into focus. In the Lozanov exercise described earlier in this book, the Spanish was the focal point of the text books, while the English translations were on the sides or in the periphery. If the student wanted to focus on them he could.

However, subliminal messages are "under the threshold" and therefore your consciousness would barely be able to discern the communication. For instance, if the language course was being done on film, and there was only one or two frames of the translation on that film, they would flash by so fast that the conscious mind would never be able to discern them.

Accelerated learning techniques avoid subliminal messages, as they are seen to constrict the mind and the personality, which the opposite of what Accelerated learning principles teach.

5. Do students immediately feel like they have learned something?

It depends on the student. Some people feel like they have learned a lot after just one session, while with others, it takes a while. As was mentioned when considering children, it is usually because there is so little effort involved that some people cannot believe they have learned anything. However, in the end, they all agree that accelerated learning works.

Conclusion

As we have seen throughout this book, our brain is amazing in its ability to pick up new skills and build information or knowledge databases. Yet even the most amazing pieces of biology need assistance once and while. Accelerated learning techniques and the memory aids that often accompany them are meant to provide that assistance.

For students, it is a chance to take charge of their own learning experience. While the teacher might provide guidance for the class and the initial concrete information to be taken in, the students themselves can provide the main focus and direction of the class or training sessions. So how can students make themselves ready for this intense learning experience?

One of the most important things that any new student can do is keep an open mind throughout the process. As we have seen during the course of the previous chapters, a positive attitude can assist any student to gain the most from their accelerated training course. Another important note is that engaging the brain and the rest of the body can assist anyone in building up their memory and skill set.

Our minds are built to take in data not in an traditional linear fashion, but in multiple layers and levels. Accelerated learning courses are made to engage with a student's mind by tackling multiple levels at the same time. As we have seen, the beauty of this type of learning is that the brain and body are both part of the process. Students can then teach others, thus reinforcing what they have already learned throughout the process of the course.

While not every learning method works for every student, accelerated learning courses do work for every learner because it can be adapted to every student's particular learning methods. Do they engage better with hands on experiences or through music and verbal imagery? Whatever works best, accelerated learning can be adapted to fit the student's specific needs.

In the end, it is important to follow the basic guideposts to create the best environment for accelerated learning to take place. Teachers who use the social aspects can find their students quickly creating a knowledge base that will provide them a long term foundation for any new skill set!

FREE BONUS #1*

A MIND FOR NUMBERS
at any age:

15 WAYS
TO EXERCISE YOUR BRAIN
TO THINK LIKE A SCIENTIST

INTRODUCTION

Scientists have long been revered for their intelligence, problem solving skills and intense knowledge. Rather than being personality traits of an individual, these attributes are actually well developed skills. This is excellent news for the average person, because it means that with practice, one can train their brain to think like a scientist.

Scientific thinking is methodical. One step follows another, and from following guided steps, one is always likely to achieve a result. This type of thinking is focused on problem solving. This involves fully understanding all the variables for a particular problem, and then analyzing these variables one at a time until a solution surfaces.

Scientists are masters of strategic thinking. In essence, strategic thinking is also methodical as it has a planning process, and added on to this is innovation, strategic planning and operational planning. Using strategies helps the scientist achieve greater success in their endeavors. They are persistent, never giving up until they finally get the desired result, and viewing every failure as an opportunity. When calculating mathematical problems, this is valuable, as when these problems increase in complexity, achieving a result becomes more difficult. The brain that is geared towards scientific thinking will never give up.

There are ten ways in which you can train your brain to think like a scientist and these are outlined as: -

1. Creating a process

2. Learn to observe

3. Infer and interpret with an educated guess

4. Practice, and the practice some more

5. Make predictions that keep you focused

6. It's all in the details

7. Unravel the contradictions

8. Be skeptical

9. Avoid thinking pitfalls

10. Seeing through scientific eyes each day

This book is designed to help you master each of these ways, thereby equipping you with excellent skills. With sufficient and consistent practice, the methods and tools that you get from this book will improve your brain activity and sharpen your focus, helping you think like a scientist.

CHAPTER ONE:
EVOLUTION OF THINKING

Before you fully dive into this book about how to think like a scientist, let's first take a look at the evolution of thinking. It'll help you understand your thinking process, as well as understand what it means to think like a scientist. We'll start with two billion years ago, when we looked nothing remotely close to a human, but were a single-celled organism.

It took us until just two million years ago for us to leave the trees for caves, and only two hundred thousand years ago until we became what are known as modern man. When language arrived is still a mystery, but an educated guess puts it as around fifty-thousand years ago. After that, it becomes a lot easier to track.

With Aristotle, around 2,500 years ago, formal logic showed up in our history. Around 400 years ago is when Francis Bacon developed the scientific method. Not long after the scientific method was invented, the Royal Society of London for Improving Natural Knowledge was created. The thinking behind these two milestones in our history was that we now knew how to define what good science was and had an organization that would monitor how science was being conducted.

The first time we used the scientific method in 1025 AD was in the 18th century when a physician known as James Lind discovered the curative properties of oranges and lemons. His discovery came about because he had used the scientific method to separate people into several groups that were randomized. He figured out that the oranges and lemons helped when treating sailors who had scurvy. He didn't have a name for the substance in the oranges and lemons that helped, but we would later call it vitamin C.

The idea of statistical thinking is still just a baby at just a little over a hundred years old. Ronald Fisher, a British statistician, brought about the use of the p-value to propose limits of chance versus significance.

The point of all this is to illustrate that we have only been thinking logically for the last 2,500 years, and we've only been able to use the scientific method for the past 400 years. In the meantime, we had to use other methods of thinking in order to survive, so what were they?

When we were living in tribes, the best thing we could do to survive was to emulate others. If our tribe mate was never ill, we would follow him or her around and mimic their every move so that we didn't become ill, too. For millions of years we honed this practice of observing a positive trait, mimicking the behaviors of those who had the traits, and repeating.

Yet we've only had 0.0002% of that time to hone our skills for logical thinking. That means when we think logically, we have to go against those millions of years of hardwired thinking of copycats. We have to fight against the very evolution that kept us alive and go out of our way to think logically and scientifically.

Since the invention of the MRI, we've been studying our brains. Neuroscientists have been wondering about the impact of independent thinking on our brains and its activity, and they've discovered some interesting tidbits of information. One of those tidbits is very provocative and interesting. Those who think logically were studied under an MRI machine while they were thinking in this manner, and the neuroscientists found that there is an actual pain of independence. The amygdalae of those who think logically were lit up and the brain was producing stress signals. Thinking logically is actually emotionally stressful; however, it's a necessary occurrence for those who want to think like a scientist.

Therefore, we're not genetically equipped to think in a logical or scientific manner because it's an evolutionary development that's still in its infancy. Many logical thinkers become frustrated that there isn't more scientific research and data in the news media; however, can we really become upset with a species that has survived doing what they're currently doing? That doesn't make mimicry correct, but it's like punishing a tree for oozing sap when its limb is cut off.

So what can you do about it?

Correcting everyone's behavior is simply not feasible and it's not necessarily the right path to choose, but you have already shown an interest in changing your path in life. You've picked up this book on logical thinking and you have a desire to learn, and this is the most paramount ingredient to success. The next ingredient is to find a mentor, and I'm hoping that I can be your first mentor with this book, but you should find another in your field of study that you can speak with in person.

CHAPTER TWO:
HOW WE EXERCISE OUR BRAINS
LIKE SCIENTISTS ON A DAILY BASIS

Did you know that we all think on a scientific basis every day? That's right, every decision you make and every though process you have about those decisions is a scientific process. I know you might not believe me, so let's take a look at some examples. This will help you think more like a scientist throughout your daily activities so that you can practice.

Observing

We have five senses that we currently know of: sight, sound, touch, taste, and hearing. When we use one or more of these senses to determine or gather information, we're making an observation. For example, you might determine that something is sharp because you poked your finger with it, or that an object is green because you're looking at it. Scientists use their five senses to determine whether things are dangerous, what their texture, shape, color, smell, and sometimes even taste are. Of course, there are some senses it would be best not to test out because some things might be poisonous, like gasoline, so they don't always use all five senses.

Scientists also use instruments in order to make their observations more thorough, such as using a microscope to determine the width or length of a hair, or a centrifuge to separate blood particles.

What matters about observation is that you can record these tidbits of information as facts and not as a guess. You know that a blade of grass is green or that the knife is sharp. You can put that information down as a fact so that you can use it later in order to help solve a problem. If you cannot say for sure the information you're gathering is a fact, then you must put it under a separate category and try to prove or disprove whether it's true.

Inferring

Once you've observed something happening or used one of your senses to determine that an object is a specific color, for example, then you need to interpret that data and make an educated guess, also known as an inference. Inferences are an interpretation that you've made of the data you've gathered, but they don't always mean you're correct. This is where most people stop when they make an assumption, but a scientist knows that they need to dig deeper.

As an example, perhaps you hear a rooster crowing before you open your eyes. From your childhood, you've learned a rooster crows in the morning, most of the time. So you make the assumption that the rooster is crowing because it's currently morning; however, you might be wrong. The rooster could be crowing because he is hurt or there is someone disturbing his sleep. Therefore, you've inferred that it's morning, but you don't really know unless you dive into the information further.

Another example might be that you hear the sound of a cat purring. You automatically assume the cat is happy, but did you know that cats will purr if they're injured or upset? Therefore, without *seeing* the cat and observing how it reacts with someone else, you don't know for sure the cat is happy.

Scientists understand that these educated guesses are valid, but they're not solid and thought out. Therefore, they need more information.

Predictions

Most of us watch a prediction on a daily basis. It's known as weather predictions. Predictions are inferences that have been made due to past events and currently evidence that matches up with those past events. We have fancy computer models to teach us all about the weather, but meteorologists are taught how to predict the weather manually so that they understand how the entire process works.

Let's use a more real-life example. Do you remember when you were a child and you stepped into the rain for the first time? Perhaps it was a cool fall rain, or maybe it was a warm, summer rain. If we see rain outside and it's autumn, we will predict that it's going to be cool rain because it was cool before when we experienced it; however, we don't really know until we step out into the rain. That's a prediction based upon past experiences and current data.

Classifying Data

Classifying data is simply grouping it together so that you can see how it relates to one another. For example, a scientist is studying three different plants. One plant has a yellow flower, the other a blue, and the final a red. He would group that information together under one category known as 'Color.' He may then take measurements of the plants leaves, and classify that data under 'Leaf Measurements.'

You might practice classification of data on a daily basis. Perhaps you are searching for information in an old yearbook and you want to find someone's picture. You first look at the grade they were in, and then you search for them by the first letter of their last name, alphabetically. This is an example of data that has been organized and classified.

Models

Do you remember playing with those tiny army men or those baby dolls when you were a child? While they were rudimentary in the fact that they might not have been to scale or they didn't have great detail, they were models. When you made a mud-pie that was smaller than a real pie, you were making a model. When you look at something on the computer screen that's a drawing of an object that will be much larger, that's a model. Even when you draw something on notebook paper, such as a tree, it's a model.

Some models can be to scale while others don't really need to be to scale. Models are great for understanding something that's very complex, such as the reproductive system or the inside of a cell in science class. The best example of a model is a solar system model that shows how the planets rotate around the sun and what color they are.

A scientist uses a model in order to simplify a complicated idea or information. They're usually generated by computers, but we used to draw models by hand on pieces of paper, and even make them with wooden sculptures when we didn't have paper.

Communication

On a daily basis you talk with your friends and family, and you listen to what others are saying, and you even write messages via e-mail, texting, or some still use snail-mail. Communication is something that every human being does, and it doesn't even have to be with other people. Sometimes we communicate with ourselves and we communicate with a pet, such as a dog we want to sit down or roll over. In order to communicate effectively, we must do more than just speak, we must also listen.

Scientists understand that we have to listen on a daily basis in order to gather, share, and form opinions about information. Then we share that information, data, results, and opinions with others in order to get *their* opinions. Scientists will use a formal method of communicating like the Internet, reports, and meetings, but they may also have informal communication between each other in the field.

As you can see, we all think like a scientist on a daily basis, at least up to the part where we observe, but a true scientist moves beyond that point. They make educated guess and then explore those guesses and turn them into truths or untruths. Then they explore further to discover more truths about their surroundings. They're always learning.

CHAPTER THREE: UNDERSTANDING THE NEED TO EXERCISE THE BRAIN

The brain controls all of our thinking, and is constantly sending messages throughout our body guiding our actions. Just like you would go to the gym to build up a muscle and improve your strength, you also need to continuously work on developing your brain to bring the most out from it.

Scientists have mastered the art of keeping their brains active, focused and in constant development. They somehow seem to increase their knowledge and reasoning over time, where most people experience diminished brain activity and capacity. When working with numbers, it is particularly important to have a brain that is 'switched on', to ensure you can get accurate results, as well as to avoid the mental taxation that can result from working out problems.

For this reason, understanding brain plasticity is key. Brain plasticity is the brains natural ability to remodel itself throughout life.

The brain is made up of one hundred billion neurons, and early on, scientists believed the ability to create new neurons ceased after birth. However, they now understand that the brain is able to reorganize itself and create fresh connections, or even create new neurons.

Think about someone who has just had a stroke. If the scientists were accurate, someone who had suffered a stroke and lost the ability to speak would not be able to regain that ability. There are many stroke victims out there who would disprove this theory that neurons are static and never-changing. Their brains were able to rewire themselves in order to allow the person to speak again.

Brain plasticity is dynamic, meaning that it's ever-changing. While for some this might be encouraging information, for others you might be thinking, but doesn't that mean it can falter at any time? Your brain's plasticity varies by your age and some changes are predominant when you're an infant, a child, and a teenager. It also involves more than just neurons. Your brain's plasticity includes other cells such as the glial and vascular cells. So their health is just as important in your brain's ability to easily rewire itself.

Another interesting fact about your brain's plasticity is that it can happen for two reasons: learning and experiences, as well as memory formation, and brain damage. The way your brain changes is not always for the better, so be aware of how you're treating it and taking care of it. Some of you might be thinking that now you know your brain is basically able to heal itself, you can abuse it. Remember that when you damage your brain, it takes a longer time to heal when you're an adult. While you still have neurons, they're not as agile as they once were.

So how does your brain keep up with everything that you learn and still retain the ability to change when you're an adult? It's a lot like trimming the dead leaves off a plant. Your brain periodically goes through all of your neurons, and the ones that have not been used the longest are the ones that are culled.

There are two different types of brain plasticity. There's functional plasticity which allows the brain to move neural pathways from a damaged part of the brain to an undamaged part of the brain. This is the type of plasticity that's in action when a person is in a car accident or has a stroke and suffers brain damage. Then there's structural plasticity, which is what we'll be focusing on in this book.

Structural plasticity is the brain's ability to restructure itself in order for you to learn. When you learn something new, your brain creates a neural pathway so that you are able to retain that information. That's the plasticity that you really want to exercise, so that you can learn easily and be fluid in your learning.

The brain is not static; it is always taking in new information, as well as releasing information. The brain is continuously taught how to pay attention, increase its functioning speed, retain memories, navigate problems, develop social or people skills and build on intelligence. In order to exercise your brain to think like a scientist, you need to be able to control and improve your basic sensory skills.

Over time, the brain begins to lose efficiency in certain roles – that is if you have not taught your brain otherwise. Some of the things that scientists have mastered include:

- Speed – They are able to think of their feet. Without exercising the brain, activities around you remain at the same pace, but your ability to process these activities will slow down.

- Brightness – Scientists have sharp minds, always ready to process information effectively. A mind that does not engage in this type of thinking starts to get tired, and also acts tired. Dealing with issues then takes longer and can be a taxing process.

- Accuracy – Scientists pay attention to detail. By doing so, they ensure that they have covered all the bases necessary to solve a problem.

- Clarity – When addressing any issue, 'noise' or 'disruption' from the outside world is inevitable. This noise can easily lead one away from the intended path. Scientists are able to discern these noises, and focus on the main problem. This means that the solution is clear and well represented, without unnecessary variables.

- Recognition – Understanding information more deeply comes naturally to scientists. They are able to look for detail, and identify relevant information.

- Recording – As scientists become more mature in their professions, they are able to control their ability to learn, and rise to the occasion. Their minds become better with age, rather than diminishing in capacity.

When working with numbers, these roles that the brain takes on are particularly important. Numbers report information, and this information is often used to draw conclusions.

CHAPTER FOUR:
CREATING A PROCESS

All mathematical calculation follows a pre-designed process. While in school, one had to memorize formulas or understand the 'method' in order to solve mathematical problems. Each step in a method was important, and if you arrived at a correct answer, without being able to explain how you got there, it was possible that your teacher would mark your answer wrong.

Your brain is also process oriented, piecing together certain steps to fulfill a purpose. For example, following a good night's sleep, you want to brush your teeth immediately after you wake up. Your brain is trained to get you to open your eyes, get out of bed, walk towards the bathroom, put toothpaste on the brush and then brush your teeth, thereby following a process. Although it may seem simple and obvious, it is not. This is only realized once a step in the process is skipped or unattainable.

Scientific thinking entails you asking certain questions when following a process. These are the '5 W's' – who, what, when, where and why. These 5 W's are excellent when solving problems, as they attempt to exhaustively offer insight on the problem. Brainstorming entails evaluating the existing situation and discussing various solutions, following which, one is chosen. The positives and negatives are then analyzed, and thereafter an informed decision is made. With practice, the brain can be trained to evaluate situations by weighing the positives and negatives, as well as considering what alternatives exist before making a final decision.

Within the steps of the process, ensure that you always ask questions. This helps you go through each step exhaustively.

The questions that could be asked include, how do I address this situation? Is there any data I have missed? Are there new ideas I can explore? Am I fully aware of all the variables? Can I build on my results? These questions differ from the 5 w's, and have more to do with state of mind. They are especially applicable when dealing with mathematical issues. To think like a scientist, question everything, as answering the questions helps you to cover all your bases.

A simple process that can exercise the brain is as follows.

- Start with writing out the problem that you are addressing as a question.

- Brainstorm with like-minded individuals to get an idea of what information you will need to help you answer the question.

- Create a plan that will help you develop or identify the information you need.

- Clearly define all factors that you will refer to, and the protocol that shall be followed for collecting the information.

- Gather the information that you need and ensure that it is from a trustworthy source as you do so. Make sure you have enough to fill in any data collection gaps that may arise.

- As you go along, you may find that you have to modify your definitions and protocols. Be open minded and allow yourself to utilize all new information.

- Present your work in a visual manner, with a chart, mind map or illustrations. It is easier to assimilate information through diagrams than it is in written text.

A normal process would usually be concluded at this point, however, a scientific process requires several more steps. Extending the questions that the brain will ask is essential to exercising the brain, and is something that scientist have perfected. The additional steps include:

- Returning to your original questions. Review your results and consider whether you have actually been effective in finding an answer. If you have not found an answer, you can then continue to analyses the data from different perspectives until you do.

- At this point, even though you may have found an answer, ask another question which is, so what? This all important additional question will help you to explore further possibilities, and reevaluate your results. Scientists cover all their bases when addressing issues. Your brain can be trained to do more than accept what is at face value. Your brain can be taught to look for variations and further analyses what appears to be a complete answer. This will be support the initial problem, by offering deeper insight and exploring novel ideas for improvement of the results.

- Evaluate your results and identify anything else the data reveals.

- Now, where do you go from here? You can decide to continue with your exploration or to accept your results.

- In any case, you need to decide what the next important steps you want to take are.

These steps reveal that for scientific thinking, you should be able to constantly push your brain. The end of a process does not necessarily mean the end of an exploration. It simply presents an opportunity to change your point of view and continue thinking.

CHAPTER FIVE:
LEARN TO OBSERVE

Observation directly relates to your consciousness and perspectives. To be able to observe, you must have the ability to look at things from another's point of view or put yourself in another's shoes. This ensures that you have an unbiased view of any situation. Observation entails viewing every aspect of your environment, and then using this information to address an issue. Observation is more than simply seeing people, situations or things and drawing conclusions. It actually entails using all five senses to get information.

The five senses are sight, sound, smell, taste and touch. They can be used all at once, or individually based on the situation being assessed. Scientists have found ways in which they can enhance these senses so that they are able to understand a problem more deeply. When exercising the brain, increasing sharpness begins with the senses. As your brain improves the clarity with which it registers information from all your sensory organs, you improve your responses and ability to store information. Scientists have developed tools that further help them to enhance their senses and review information. For example, in order to see an object more clearly, a scientist will use a microscope. This brings to life parts of the object by allowing for a more detailed view, thereby improving the scientist's sense of sight. Other non-physical tools can be developed. Take for example sound. When having a conversation, we hear each other's voices as we exchange information and possibly some background noise like birds chirping or vehicles moving. One can then draw a basic conclusion as to the location of the conversation, whether those conversing were male or female, and even their approximated age.

A scientist will observe things more deeply. To think like a scientist, you cannot take any aspect of the conversation for granted. A scientist would listen to all the background noises, and may be able to provide additional details such as whether there was anyone else in the room. They are attuned to paying attention to detail, and amplifying those details to explore additional solutions.

As the brain registers this information from our sensory organs more clearly, we are then better able to respond to the information and store it. The ability of the brain to retain information is worth highlighting here. When working with numbers, one must remember methodologies and formulas so as to work out a problem. Having highly attuned sensory organs makes it easier to remember all aspects necessary to address the problem. Without all these in mind, it may prove impossible to resolve a mathematical issue.

When evaluating a mathematical problem for example, how can you use observation to your advantage? You can teach your brain to register details, looking beyond the surface problem to deeper understand how the numbers work. Missing details is the main cause of errors and confusion which then limits both your results and your thinking. In fact, brains that miss details often have been found to slow down, basically so that the brain can avoid making further mistakes.

When observing, results must be reported accurately and factually. Our brains have ways that they interpret information, and when we report results, they are usually peppered with our own opinions, understanding and internal references. To think like a scientist, you must be objective, and avoid bias.

Once you begin to actively observe, you will find that you are inundated with information that features many details. If you want to think like a scientist, you must learn how to pay attention to the details which matter, and refuse to focus on the details that do not matter. This is particularly important when working with numbers, so as to save you time and other resources, and also, so as to ensure that you do not use the wrong information when trying to work out a solution.

When observing, you must also be sure of the source of your information. Scientists have a keen sense when it comes to verification of their sources, as in many cases they are dealing with sensitive information.

Do not underestimate the power of the subconscious mind. Scientists operate at a high level of consciousness about the world around them. As they take in information, they are able to refer to it in the future, even though they may not have the need to use all the information they have at the present moment. With the passage of time, their subconscious mind, and level of consciousness increase in order to process more information. Scientists are able to assimilate information more deeply than the regular person, because they consciously tap into their subconscious mind to explore scenarios. When one walks into a room, you might observe the furniture, paintings and wall color. If you have succeeded in exercising your brain, you will also remember the finer details like the items on tables, temperature of the room and whether the window was open or not.

CHAPTER SIX:
INFER AND INTERPRET WITH AN EDUCATED GUESS

Scientists are curious about how things work. One of the ways that they are able discover so much about things is their curiosity to understand the world around them. To satisfy their curiosity, they ask questions that intend to discover detailed information, rather than just understand the surface cause of an issue. They try to understand different phenomena, methodologies, systems and models by breaking them down into variables and assessing each variable. They are able to turn the bigger picture, into several smaller pictures. Scientists look for possible reasons and explanations to the phenomena that they are investigating. This is most easily done by developing a hypothesis. A hypothesis is a statement which, when answered, will prove or disprove a condition under investigation.

When creating and evaluating a hypothesis, a scientist ensures that they do so from a factual point of view, not an emotional or opinionated one. Every person has biases. To be able to think like a scientist, you must be able to identify and confront your personal biases. Without this, it is highly likely that you will taint your results, and they will not be reliable. Teach yourself how to take you out of the equation whenever you are addressing a problem, and it will be easier to follow existing guidelines, formulas or methods of working out the issue.

Once you have defined your hypothesis, you can achieve results by testing it. A scientist would first create a control test, which is one where the variables do not change. The scientist then attempts to get results by applying different variables and observing the results.

When working with numbers, this system of achieving results is thorough, as you are able to review all the alternatives. Scientists use three methods when making an educated guess, and these are, inductive, deductive and causal reasoning. To exercise your brain, when presented with a problem, look at it from as many angles as possible. For example, you could assess what caused the problem, investigate the problem and identify the reasons that may arise, or what the solution to the problem is, working backwards to understand how the problem arose, or whether the problem is created by an internal or external force.

Once you have gone through making your educated guess, an investigation can be conducted and data analyzed. From the information generated, you will then be ready to draw a solid conclusion and share your results. Your solid conclusion will be as a result of your brain working with facts, and being able to assess those facts from various points of view, thereby eliminated unnecessary information or inconclusive scenarios. Factual thinking is also more reliable, as it is easier to rationalize and explain your point of view.

In addition to being factual, a scientist also uses their imagination to idealize methods to attain their results. Imagination increases the realm of possibility, and opens up the mind to finding different ways to address any issue. By tapping into your imagination, you can unleash your creativity thereby allowing your brain to assimilate information and identify the bigger picture. Looking at the bigger picture allows your brain to open itself up to endless problem solving possibilities.

CHAPTER SEVEN:
PRACTICE, AND THEN PRACTICE SOME MORE

Scientists experiment. Experimenting means that they try and try and try to solve a particular problem in as many ways as possible until they get a result. Giving up is not an option. Emotions are processed in the brain, and guide human behavior. In a situation where someone is working on an experiment or problem, and they are unable to find the solution, frustration is usually the result. Following which, the individual may simply give up because it is too difficult to find a solution. Scientists have developed the skill of taking each mistake or failure as an opportunity to search deeper for another answer. The mistake is simply a variable that is eliminated, and another course of action is taken.

To teach your brain not to 'shut down' or 'give up' when facing a problem, you must develop the scientific skill of practice, practice and then practice some more. When something is not right, therein lies the opportunity to keep working on it until it comes together. You must eliminate from your mind the word failure, and look at each instance where you do not attain a result as an opportunity. Failure is a prerequisite of success and a learning process that brings you close to your ultimate goal. Sometimes failure does not come about because of getting the wrong result, but because of a lack of persistence.

Since there is every possibility that a scientist will not achieve the result being searched for during an experiment, the scientist has to be open to receiving alternative suggestions from peers or colleagues, to expand their view and see the bigger picture. A scientist is able to choose a situation that will change his perspective. This will help in the development of more theories. Our brains are geared towards being right, and believing in our own achievements. That is why it is often difficult for us to ask for help, or even to admit when we are wrong and graciously accept correction. To think like a scientist, we need to reevaluate how we react to situations where someone is giving us correction. If your reaction is anger or displeasure, when it happens, stop. Listen to the correction, and separate fact from emotion. The brain can be trained to listen and assimilate information, rather than to listen and react. However, it will entail a conscious effort on your part to track your emotions, and change your reactions.

A busy brain is a productive brain. Ensure that your brain is being challenged with various scenarios and solution approaches. Scientists work tirelessly to produce results, and will continue to tackle a problem until they do so. If you are not familiar with continued practice, it may seem very challenging to keep your mind constantly busy. What you could do to get yourself to that point, would be to keep a detailed journal of everything you are dealing with. The journal should include details on daily observations, as well as how far you have moved forward, what your future plans are and anything else that is relevant to resolving your issue. It is important to maintain this every day for optimal results.

To stimulate the brain, you need to read constantly, and like scientists, this will create a skill that keeps your brain active. Not only is reading excellent for improving brain function, it is also great for gathering information.

Writing things down is a sure method to 'wake up' for the brain. When you write things down, you are able to work through a problem step by step, until you have written down the solution. Your brain can process information faster and with more accuracy when things are written down.

An important part of practice and thinking like a scientist involves rest. Once you have stimulated your brain, and are constantly thinking about different methodologies to address an issue, you must take a break and rest. Like any muscle in the body, a brain can get stressed leading to headaches or migraines or other health issues. The brain also requires time to rejuvenate itself in order to be continuously productive. Once you rest your brain, you are able to focus more clearly. Your brain is then able to connect unrelated factors in new ways. Some simple ways of resting the brain include taking a walk, looking out at the sun, meditation, exercise or sitting calmly with no distractions.

Finally, scientists are passionate about what they are doing and this passion drives them to think differently and deeper than the ordinary person. When training your brain to think like a scientist, you must have the innate passion to find out information. This makes it easier for your brain to process information, as you become naturally receptive. Scientists enjoy what they do, and once they have made a breakthrough, they celebrate. So in addition to working hard, focusing, continuous practice, keeping your brain busy and resting, enjoyment and celebration is also essential to stimulate the brain.

CHAPTER EIGHT:
MAKE PREDICTIONS THAT
KEEP YOU FOCUSED

Predicting a future occurrence is important when attempting to understand the occurrence, as well as the steps that are necessary to lead up to it. Scientists predict future occurrences, in order to change the circumstances around these occurrences, leading to a better result.

The way they do it is by using observations which give first-hand information, and leaning on their existing knowledge. They base their predictions on current evidence as well as previous experiences. The brain can learn how to make predictions, by understand that past behavior is a good predictor of future behavior.

If a variable behaves a certain way several times in one situation, it will continue to do so. Unless some changes are made to the process, the results are likely to be the same. Making predictions creates awareness, and helps the brain develop alternatives to issues that may be addressed.

An easy way that this can be done is mentally classifying variables so that they are easier to address. Scientists create numerous classifications when addressing problems, such as dividing their population based on similarities like age, size, color, purpose and so on. This makes it easier to understand how individuals or items connect or relate to each other.

From this, scientists are able to create models which help them to understand complex situations in simple ways. Instructions on steps to be taken can be given, and when followed, these can lead to a specific result. It is easy to teach your brain how to do this. For example, you want to assemble a DIY cupboard that you have bought. You open the box, and using the instructions, are able to put together all the pieces in a specified order so that the final result is a table.

Also, combining classifications and reviewing the effects is often done by scientists, as they seek to understand changes in the environment. When faced with a problem that has more than one variable, you can try to review what the answers would be based on combining and comparing the results.

Making connections between seemingly dissimilar concepts could bring about a breakthrough. When thinking like a scientist, you should consider what the bridge or connection could be between variables that are highly unlikely to go together.

When making a prediction, you can visualize your end result. As a problem solving tool, visualization is quite effective. Look at your dilemma as you would a picture, and where possible use diagrams to analyses it. Diagrams are easier to understand than text, especially if several pages of data can be illustrated on a single page diagram. Your brain will be able to view the diagram, and also try to understand what may be causing the issue. Visualization also makes it easier to see the whole picture, and consider the available options.

CHAPTER NINE:
IT'S ALL IN THE DETAILS

Scientists are masters of dissecting the details of a problem. That is why you can present them with three or four variables requesting for their insight and feedback, and receive pages worth of information on how those variables affect each other. It is important to them to look further than the surface, and to search deeply into the reasons that a certain phenomenon is occurring. To think like a scientist and develop an eye for detail, you can try using a control test.

When carrying out experiments, the control test is key as it becomes the main reference point for all the other tests. The control test is a test that has no variables. It is also known as the main test and is used as for comparison with all the other results. Take for example you are baking a batch of cookies, and want to evaluate how changes in ingredients will affect the final result. You would start with a standardized recipe, which would be your control test. To start, you would follow your standard recipe and take note of the results. These results could include cooking time, final look, texture, flavor and so on. Using the same standardized recipe that you started with, you add or take away ingredients to produce new batches, and you should become aware of how these changes affect the original recipe. By noting each change, you have an idea of how a variation in a detail can change the final output. As a scientist, it is essential that you keep track of any information you receive.

You can utilize the same principle when you are dealing with numbers. In fact, you will find that this is the methodology used in algebra or for basic problem solving. Once you are aware of a standard formula, the "control test" of your mathematical problem, you can then use the formula, adding variations as you go along to suit the conditions of the problem. For example, you may be working on payroll information, trying to evaluate how to justify increasing the salaries of certain employees. When everyone joins the organization at a certain level, they all receive the same salary. In order to justify the increases, you can give value to certain elements, for example always meeting targets, increasing revenue, diversifying portfolio, improving your education or qualifications and so on. It is these little details that need to be logically and strategically assessed, so that any increases in salary are not only backed by fact, but can easily be justified, evaluated and measured.

When scientists use this technique, they make sure to test as many variables as possible because by doing so, they are able to achieve a more thorough answer. It is possible to get your brain to work in a similar manner by considering all possible scenarios and their likely outcomes. Once you have done so, you can make an informed decision based on your available information.

CHAPTER TEN:
UNRAVEL THE CONTRADICTIONS

Just as no two people are the same, a mathematical problem may be solved using two different methodologies, yet the answers will be exactly the same. This often time has people believe that there is evidence of contradictions, or that they are dealing with a paradoxical situation. In fact, a heated debate on methodology and similar findings can make solving mathematical riddles both stressful and contentious.

When thinking like a scientist, this is the sort of situation that should peak your interest and in effect get your creative juices flowing. A situation which presents contradicting information allows for investigation that goes to the heart of the matter, where you follow logical steps and possibly use a check list to ensure that you have covered all of your bases. It also allows the scientists to think outside of the box, especially if a situation arises where one of the methodologies needs to be properly justified. Scientists are always interested in looking at two or more well established findings that appear to contradict each other for various reasons.

Opening Up the Possibilities in the Mind

1. The first reason is they need to think outside the box. Despite having extensive problem solving knowledge, and being equipped with rich skills to address a range of situations, scientist are still able to admit that they do not know it all. These contradictory situations present them with opportunities to delve into the unknown, increase their knowledge and find their way around a mystery or misunderstood criterion. By thinking outside the box, they ensure that their brains are always receptive to learning new

ideas and improved methods of thinking. They are willing to consider radical approaches to problem solving so that they can fully understand contradictory methodologies. When working with numbers this becomes vital. Maintaining a rigid stance in regards to how one can reach a result or reviewing alternative types of evaluations may negatively limit the problem solver, putting them at a disadvantage with others. The constantly changing and improving methodologies in mathematics needs people with brains that are more open minded and willing to accept change.

Suspending Judgment

2. The second reason is that unravelling contradictions helps to suspend judgments. A good scientist does not think of a problem as right or wrong, rather the approach could be why or why not. Judgment should not be made on the methodology or the outcome until everything has been done and it is the conclusion that is being reviewed or addressed. Evaluating contradictions helps the scientist assess deep conceptual and analytic foundations that are affecting the conflicting conclusions or methodologies. When these evaluations are done without any judgment, it helps the scientist review evidence through a new lens. For brain development, this is essential as it helps avoid developing habits in thinking and assessment. A habit is difficult to break, and greatly limits the thinkers ability to see beyond the habit. Once you have taught your brain to use a single set of criteria to assess a situation, it becomes a real challenge to even consider alternatives. Suspending judgment is akin to keeping an open mind at all time to allow for the consideration of a range of alternatives.

Cast a Wide Net for New Ideas

3. The third reason is so that you can cast a wide net for new ideas and supporting evidence. Reviewing contradictions should help your brain consider information that may have previously been nonsensical. This is because you are able to review more solutions that the potentially obvious. By casting a wide net, you may opt to review other fields, consider cross disciplinary research or attempt to try a few way of dealing with arising issues. When working with numbers, this strategy will make it easier for you to remain up to date with the latest findings on addressing issues. On top of that, your brain will be able to develop new ideas as it goes through unfamiliar information, and you should gain valuable insight that will allow new patterns of thinking to emerge.

Sometimes when you begin to unravel the contradictions, you may establish that these contradictions exist as they reside in different disciplines. Mathematically, this can help you understand why methodologies may be different for the same issue. Take for example the calculation of IRR (Internal Rate of Return). It is used in financial management for the time value of money, as well as in project management to ascertain the validity of the project. In both disciplines, the answers may be the same, although the methodology used and the explanation for the steps used may be as different as night and day. However, you can teach your brain to understand the differences in the methodologies so that they can be used where appropriate. This trains the brain to explore areas outside of what is expected, to enable the unravelling of the contradictions.

CHAPTER ELEVEN:
BE SKEPTICAL

According to Nobel Prize winning physicist Richard Feynman, "You must not fool yourself as you are the easiest person to fool." This statement is highly significant when referring to the workings of your brain. The human brain can be "arrogant". Often when we know a little, we believe we know a lot. The issue with this is that we then begin to limit our ability to assimilate new information, because after all, if we know so much what more is there for us to learn. This causes us to create behaviors and thinking patterns that revolve around just what we know, creating a situation where we become set in our ways for taking action. Once we master a particular way of doing things, we may practice it until we get it perfect, inadvertently limiting ourselves to new learnings.

As a normal person, you are vulnerable to believing information without using deep logic or having proper evidence. As long as it is seems to make sense, is accepted by a large group of people, or is spoken out by someone that you respect, you will take certain information to be fact or real. If you are asked for any evidence, you would gladly quote your sources, although unbeknownst to you, they may be highly unreliable. However, once you train your brain to think like a scientist that ceases to be the case.

Scientists are sceptics, meaning that they take time to question their beliefs. Therefore, if you present a scientist with a result or a situation, the first thing that they are likely to do is research to ensure that things are as they have been presented. Whereas a normal person would have their brain hardwired to having their beliefs come first and their explanation for the belief second, the scientific mind would have an opposite system. For example, a normal person thinking could believe that driving fast will cause a car accident, because one would lose control of the car. The belief here is that driving fast will cause an accident, whereas the explanation would be losing control of the car. The scientist would view this problem working from the end result to the belief. The first point that would be addressed is from viewing the wreckage, what caused the accident? Following which, the belief is established so as to explain what led to the accident.

When working with numbers, this would mean that even though you know an answer is correct, you need to offer evidence of its viability first and foremost. Take the car example above, the assumption of speeding causing the accident should be backed up by skid marks on the road, torn tires or any other relevant evidence. By reviewing all this evidence together, it should then be possible to paint a picture of what really happened. Therefore, you are likely to emphasize your methodology much more than your answer. In fact, in some cases you may find that you have arrived at the wrong answer, but because you used the right methodology, you are confident that you have done the right thing. Thinking like a scientist does not mean that you get it right every time. It means that you should be open to new learning.

Being skeptical applies to our own biases. Our brains are skilled at identifying the cognitive biases in other people's thinking, but may not do so when it comes to our own. This basically means that we trust our opinions deeply, and find it hard to question or justify them. Therefore if you believe the sky is blue and someone told you that it was green, you would likely object and not even bother with an explanation of your stance. However, if you were referring to a journal article on the same supposition, you are more likely to argue on that person's thinking. When thinking like a scientist, we need to be open to our own biases, so that we can question and address them to acquire more knowledge. Rather than accept our thinking as fast, firm and authoritative, thinking like a scientist demands that we can back up our opinions using reliable sources. It entails taking some time to logically arrange thoughts.

Skepticism is in essence, a reward for the scientific mind. It allows you to avoid the pitfalls of human nature so that when facing any problem, you can view it with a clear vision and eventually arrive at the truth of the matter. In addition, skepticism allows your brain to carry out a rational inquiry. This means that before you arrive at an answer, you systematically go through all the existing alternatives, eliminating those that are unnecessary and emphasizing those which are helpful. A rational inquiry means that you can see subjects from a scientific perspective, which can be particularly helpful when dealing with mathematical problems. This is because you will view a sequence or process, helping you move through the problem one step at a time. It involves making arguments based on logical steps and strategy.

Take for example, the work of an auditor. An auditor's job is to check on the books of a business, ensuring that the numbers that have been provided match with available information. The auditor usually works from the end result backwards, in an attempt to confirm or justify the result. Being skeptical and questioning irregularities is important for this position. However, to be effective, these questions need to be addressed in a logical manner, based entirely on the information provided and with no biases from previous experiences. This clarity of thought based on scientific reasoning will help the auditor arrive at a clear and reliable conclusion.

CHAPTER TWELVE: AVOID THINKING PITFALLS

The previous chapter addresses the way that we can use skepticism to understand how our brains work to form beliefs. However, our brains can also lead us astray where we experience certain pitfalls due to our thoughts. When this happens, we as people form bad or invalid arguments in favor of our beliefs. When working with numbers, especially in finance, these thinking pitfalls can lead to you deceiving yourself rather than using your mind to propel yourself forward. There are four thinking pitfalls that can be avoided if you use scientific reasoning and these are: -

1) **Coincidences** – This is nothing more than the laws of probability in action. Probability is simply the extent to which an event is likely to occur, measured by the ratio of the favorable cases to the whole number of cases possible.

   When an event occurs, if it seems to be out of place, different from the norm or even a phenomenon it may be seen as a coincidence. The scientific mind does not accept coincidences. Instead, probability is assessed to evaluate the likelihood of the event occurring, supported by evidence or a detailed explanation.

2) **The Either/Or Phenomenon** – As human beings we like to make simple choices. This means that if presented with a range of variables, our thinking is focused on only those variables. We try to make choices based on what is presented before us. Mathematically this can be limiting and shows an inability to think outside the box. The scientific mind uses alternative reasoning. It avoids viewing the world in such a

way that you need to discredit one position and are then forced to accept the other positions. Scientists teach their brains to understand that reasoning more than either/or, that there is also the option "maybe".

3) **After the Fact Reasoning** – This basically refers to the type of superstition that attributes an outcome to a previous action. As human beings, we often have strange beliefs which we view as cause and effect. For example attributing hit marks in an examination to the fact that you used a lucky pencil. Scientists avoid this type of reasoning and have taught their brains to review things logically and systematically. This is particularly significant when analyzing numbers to get results, as any conclusion needs to be based on facts and suppositions.

4) **Tautology and Redundancy** – When starting an investigation, you may develop a hypothesis or a premise for testing. If your conclusion or claim is simply a restatement of one of the premises or hypothesis, then it is said to be redundant. Scientific thinking entails detailed investigation. It needs for the scientist to work out a reason as to the conclusion. In mathematical thinking, redundancy would be akin to starting with your formula as both the questions and the answer. It reveals minimal effort made and a lack of creativity. The brain needs to be directed towards being focused on problem solving so as to avoid redundancy.

In addition to these four thinking pitfalls are other factors that distort precepts and lead us to resist other viewpoints. This way, we become unable to open up our minds and explore the methods and benefits of scientific thinking. These are known as biases. The following are some common biases that are seen in everyday life.

Confirmation Bias

This can be defined as the tendency to interpret new evidence as confirmation of one's existing beliefs or theories. When thinking like a scientist, it is very easy to fall for this particular bias. The reason being that often times, you gather a range of variables and want them to makes sense together more than anything. This could possible make it easier for you to explain a certain result or justify some existing work. Therefore, instead of doing a thorough investigation, conclusions are accepted because they fit in with opinions. When working with numbers, the brain must think scientifically in order to avoid this bias. The reason being that different scenarios may call for different results, which can only be ascertained if a step by step strategic process is followed. As confirmation bias to some extent relies on assumption, you may receive the wrong results and experience difficulty trying to correct mistakes brought on by this bias.

Attribution Bias

This bias is defined as a cognitive bias that refers to the systematic errors made when people evaluate or try to find reasons for their own and others' behaviors. When conducting any type of research, it is imperative to carry out the study and let the results reveal themselves. When you have an attribution bias, it means that you look at a behavior or a result, and attempt to explain why it is so, without following the proper research steps to prove it. The problem here is that sometimes what is being investigated is not affected by the investigating attributes. Therefore, to think scientifically one should keep away from this bias. Instead, research should be conducted thoroughly, with all results being based on the actual findings.

Mathematically, this would mean that you have worked out a problem and received an answer which may or may not be correct. However, you then go about trying to justify why the response is what it is, instead of offering a proper detailed outline of how you arrived at the answer.

Agreement Bias

Cognitive dissonance, it sounds like some kind of disease that the human brain has, and in a way, it is. We all have preferences when it comes to politics, foods, music, clothing, and anything else that we actually have a choice in, which is pretty much everything. We don't like it when our preferences are challenged or when our viewpoints are challenged, and thus we stick with websites and other people who share the same viewpoints and opinions we do in order to avoid confrontation and the questioning of our beliefs.

This bias is dangerous because it keeps up from seeing the entire issue at hand or the entire world, really. We shut ourselves off from that which makes us uncomfortable and end up missing quite a lot of interesting and relevant data.

As a real world example, let's say you're a man or a woman who will only date a potential life partner who also likes Italian food and hates sushi. You pass up on anyone who is eating out at a sushi bar or anyone who won't order spaghetti at a restaurant, which are quite a few people. You may be passing up a life partner that is ultimately very good for you because they open your horizons to new foods and adventures, and you might be very, very happy with them in the future.

So you see, sticking with only your beliefs and your preferences can be detrimental to your relationship with others.

In-group Bias

Just as we're bias toward the people we love such as family members and friends, we're negatively bias toward those we don't know, such as a stranger who moves in next door or a person who want to join a specific group. In the olden days, this may have kept up safe from a stranger trying to infiltrate our tribe and cause trouble, but now that we're a global community that needs to let go of those differences and learn to work together.

This bias actually has a lot to do with our brain chemistry, believe it or not. When we're in a group of people we know and trust, our brains release a neurotransmitter known as oxytocin, also known as the love molecule. It makes us feel good and helps us form strong bonds with those around us. Unfortunately, the same neurotransmitter also makes us feel fearful and suspicious of those who attempt to infiltrate our familiar group.

While this is helpful for everyday interactions with strangers because we don't want to become prey to a predator, we also need to understand this is happening to us when we're in business meetings or in a scientific group.

Gambler's Fallacy

It's known as a fallacy but it's actually a miscommunication in our brain. The gambler's fallacy or bias is what makes a gambler keep gambling, and often brings about the gambling addiction. For example, you've flipped a coin thirty times in a row and it's all come up with heads, so we automatically keep going because we believe that soon it has to be tails because the odds are in our favor. However, this isn't the case with statistics. The odds are still 50/50 each time the coin is flipped. The odds don't change depending upon how many times you flip the coin because it resets every time you flip that coin. Therefore, the outcome is statistically independent and the probability of the outcome is still the same.

There's also the positive expectations bias, which is highly related to the gambling addiction problem. It's the idea that eventually our luck will change, either for the better or for the good. Statistically, however, our luck remains the same each time we roll a dice or play Blackjack. It's also the same feeling we get when we begin a new relationship and believe that it will be better than the previous one. In reality, all the odds are reset every time we do something.

A scientist understands this and uses statistics in their observations. They allow themselves to not fall into the trap of gambling when they're researching a hypothesis, and they recognize when they're starting to slip.

Post-Purchase Rationalization

We've all done this and there isn't anything to be ashamed about when it comes to having this bias, but we need to recognize when we're experiencing it. If you want to think like a scientist on a daily basis, you have to not only recognize and work on avoiding scientific bias, but also the biases that make us human.

As an example, the post-purchase rationalization bias is one that affects us all when we buy something we know is a bad decision. Yet after we purchase it, we rationalize that we needed it in some way and make ourselves believe that it was a good idea all along. For instance, say you purchase a vehicle that you know you can't afford in the long-run, but you somehow obtained a loan for it. A few months later, you're still rationalizing that you needed that vehicle even though you have buyer's remorse because deep down, you know you could have bought a cheaper one.

We're subconsciously justifying our purchasing decisions.

Neglecting Probability

People have a tendency to overinflate something that is actually not that dangerous compared to underinflating their reactions to something that is *that* dangerous. For example, we tend to be more afraid of getting into an airplane than getting into a vehicle, even when we logically know that our chances of dying in a car crash are much greater than the odds of dying in a plane crash. Statistically, we're more likely to die in a vehicular accident with the odds of 1 in 84 compared to a chance of 1 in 5,000 in an airplane crash.

We're also more afraid of a terrorist attack than we are of dying from falling down the stairs or an accidental poisoning, which are both far more likely to occur than a terrorist attack.

This is known as probability neglect. We are not able to grasp a good sense of risk or peril properly and thus fear things that we shouldn't compared to things that we really ought to. This leads us to overstate a risk and the probability of becoming injured, and understate a risk that is more likely to injure or kill us.

Scientists understand and observe themselves doing this when they're investigating information. We're more likely to be afraid of the brightly colored frog than we are of the dull colored one, but in reality, the dull one might be more poisonous. That's why we investigate our theories by testing information and making our observations into truths or untruths. It's better to know for sure.

Observational Selection Bias

Have you ever noticed that when you start listening to a particular band or you start wearing a particular colored shirt, you notice more and more people wearing that that shirt or listening to that band? This is known as observational selection bias. For some reason our brains focus on things that are similar to us or focus on something because we're fascinated with it.

The truth is these things are actually not occurring at a different rate. Very rarely is that true. Our brains are just fixated on that object or phenomenon, and we seem to notice it more often. We start to believe that this isn't a coincidence, which can become very disconcerting for some.

Scientists don't automatically believe that something is happening more often just because they saw it once and their brains fixated on it. They study these occurrences and build solid proof that something is happening more often. As a scientific example, let's say scientists discover a new illness, but in reality it's actually not new. It's been around for centuries, but they just didn't have the tools to diagnose it. Now they have the tools to do so. Some of them might fall into the trap of thinking that this not so new illness is happening more often, but in reality it's just that they're able to see it now.

Status-Quo Bias

People tend to be very apprehensive about chance, and this leads to us making a choice or choices that guarantee our current status-quo stays the same or change very little. This can have very many negative effects on our daily lives as well as our long-term lives. It's often seen in politics and economics, especially in the United States government. For example, many people are in favor of the universal healthcare act; however, they're not supportive of it when they find out it means their healthcare status may change, even if it's for the better.

Scientists understand that every day things change, and they step back from a situation and view it from a logical standpoint rather than an emotional one. They might ask themselves things such as, will this make a positive or negative difference in my life or the life of someone else? Will this make a positive or negative impact on the outcome of my experiment? They don't allow their emotions to come into play.

Negativity Bias

Have you ever heard someone say that when they're passing a card accident on the highway they slow down and gawk, even though they really don't want to see anything bad? We're more apt to pay attention to bad news than we are good, but why is this? Are we morbid? Do we want to see other suffer? It's really not as bad as it might seem.

The reason we want to pay special attention to negative things happening is because we want to make sure those negative things don't affect us. For example, we turn on the news every night and look at plenty of horrible stories happening, and we're glad that we're safe and comfortable in our own homes. At least, we perceive ourselves to be safe.

While this was great for us in the past, it's not becoming detrimental to our society. Scientists argue that violence is actually declining while most of the general public would argue that it's on the rise. Why? Because they tend to pay attention to all of the negative publicity and newscasters know this, so they put up more bad stories than they do good.

Scientists understand that they cannot focus solely on the bad during an experiment. They know that there are good outcomes and that not everything is negative.

Bandwagon Effect

Most people are not conscious of the fact that they actually love to go along with the flow of a crowd. When we're at a baseball game or we're at the racetrack betting on horses, we always switch our rooting for the team that's winning or the team that everyone around us is rooting for. We start to groupthink or think in the mentality of a hive. It actually doesn't have to be a large crowd, though. Sometimes we behave this way when we're in a small group, even a family group.

The bandwagon effect or group bias is what often creates behaviors that are known as social norms, and memes to propagate amongst groups of individuals. There is no evidence or support for the way a group behaves, but they behave that way because it's acceptable. Scientists are aware of this type of thinking and they're very conscious of when they might be participating in it.

A scientist comes up with a theory of their own and only agrees with another scientist when there is evidence pointing to the both of them being correct. They sometimes slip up and will participate in groupthink, but they're aware of it when it occurs and are able to step back and think more logically.

Projection Bias

Have you ever been with someone and they agreed with every word you said, and you believed them when they agreed with you? Then you find out later they talked about the same subject with someone else and their reasons were completely against what you had both agreed on in the first place? This is known as projection bias. We oftentimes believe we're right and think that others believe us to be right without asking their opinion.

In some cases, we also believe that what is best for us is best for someone else. For example, have you ever had a relative that told you to take a certain course or path in college or life, only to find out later they had wished they'd done what they'd told you to do when they were younger? They believe that you should complete the same things they wanted to do in order for you to be a good and successful person. This happens very often with children and parents when the children are looking for a college and trying to determine what they want to do for a living.

The Current Moment Bias

When given the choice, human beings will choose pleasure for the current moment and push off experiencing pain or discomfort for later rather than just get it over with. In a study conducted in 1998, scientists discovered this phenomenon by offering the participants chocolate or fruit for that day, and had them make the decision of what they were going to eat the following week. Seventy-four percent of the participants chose to eat the chocolate that day and push off eating the fruit the following week.

How much do you want to bet they would have don't he same thing on a daily basis until that week that had been in the future was up, and they hadn't eaten fruit?

Scientists recognize when they're putting something off because they know it will cause them some sort of discomfort, whether it's emotional, mental, or physical, and they stop pushing that inevitability off to another day.

Anchoring Effect

The anchoring effect or the relativity trap is the tendency to compare and contrast a limited set of items rather than looking at the overall picture. People start to fixate on one value or number that becomes compared with everything else.

For example, say you're at a store and you see a sale item. We see the difference in price and we value that, but we don't see the overall price itself. That's why most restaurants will feature an expensive entrée and then include a more reasonably priced one, but it's actually not really reasonably priced.

So now that you recognize biases, how do you get past them?

Hindsight Bias

The final bias to watch out for is the hindsight bias, which is known as the knew it all along effect or creeping determinism, and it is the inclination, after an event has occurred, to see the event as having been predictable, despite there having been little or no objective basis for predicting it. This happens when you are working and have already got a predetermined idea of the result, so much so that when you get it you can exclaim, "You see. I knew it." The problem with the hindsight bias is once you get the results, you close your mind to further evaluation and determining whether it was possible to get some more information. A scientist never allows this to happen, as even at the end of the experiment, they do not view the end, rather they are interested in the possibilities for the future. So results are rarely viewed as predictable, and in addition, are not predicted during the testing phases.

CHAPTER THIRTEEN: SEEING THROUGH SCIENTIFIC EYES EACH DAY

This book is designed to explain how you can exercise your brain to think like a scientist every day. However, you may be surprised to note that in addition to the advice and techniques that you have read so far, you have already been exercising your brain, and are ingrained with the tools to think like a scientist.

Thinking like a scientist, or training the brain towards scientific thinking is all about methodology before you arrive at a conclusion, you will try a new way of figuring things out by looking at the situation, offering an explanation and observing its effectiveness. What makes scientific thinking different from normal thinking is the element of strategy. A strategy does not only refer to a scenario where high powered executives meet to make decisions, it also refers to the basic act of creating a plan.

As you can tell, this is simple and does not require a complex set of skills. However, when one thinks of thinking like a scientist to analyze numbers, it may seem daunting or even complex. Here are a few ways that we use science on a daily basis. By understanding them, we can teach our brains how to apply scientific thinking to more situations, especially how we deal with numbers.

The Crossword Puzzle

Completing crossword puzzles is like competing with mental acrobatics. The same methods you would use here apply to scientific problems, as well as mathematical ones. To start, you look at the clue in the puzzle and evaluate whether you understand it or not. If you understand the clue, you make a guess at the word that is meant to fit in the blanks. If you do not understand the clue or cannot figure out the answer, you skip this clue hoping that as you fill in more blanks, the solution will come to you. Scientists draw conclusions in the same way. They have trained their brains to think about clues so as to fill in the blanks in their experiments or work, and when they do not know the answer, they address other variables to draw inspiration. This is an activity that millions of people all over the world engage in on a daily basis. It encourages scientist thinking through rational, elimination and strategy.

Using a Recipe to Cook a Meal

If you have ever observed a seasoned chef at work, you will observe a combination of artistic and scientific thinking. The artistic thinking is revealed in the beauty of presentation, whereas the scientific thinking is present in the balancing of flavors.

Like a crossword puzzle, cooking begins with a guess that two ingredients will work together to produce something delicious. Once the ingredients are put together, they chef tastes the meal to see if all the ingredients have come together correctly. If it is not right, different elements are added until a balance is found. Cooking needs logical thought and many people use this reasoning on a daily basis. Mathematical problems can also have these elements, whereby if your answer is not right, you try working it out with various options until you receive the desired result.

Handling Repairs

You need to have a certain level of scientific reasoning and strategy to make repairs to your car or your plumbing for example. You start of by guessing the source of the problem. At this juncture, you need to go into the actual car or walls if it plumbing and ensure that you have been able to find the source of the problem. The reason that you are guessing is that it might sometimes not be clear. If you are able to find the source, then you can go ahead and finalize the repairs. If you have not found the source then you can begin trying out a solution (or range of solutions, eliminating those that do not work along the way) and seeing if it works. When working with numbers, you can apply these principles to get to your final answer. By narrowing down and eliminating the alternatives that do not provide answers, you can reach the right conclusion.

If you observe these examples, you will notice three main similarities that apply for scientific thinking. The first is guessing at the problem, the second is reviewing and trying the alternatives and finally checking to see if the solution worked. Working with numbers is relatively simple if you apply these principles to get you proposed output. The simplicity of teaching your brain to think scientifically is amazing. The word science need not be associated with complexity and difficulty. Perhaps being a professional scientist can be realistically viewed as difficult, but practicing scientific thinking on a daily basis is something we do easily even without realizing that we are.

CHAPTER FOURTEEN: HOW TO OVERCOME BIASES

Now that you know biases exist, you're one step closer to overcoming them both in your daily life and in your logical thinking exercises that you perform both in school and in a scientific setting.

Recognizing the Bias

The first step to overcoming a bias is knowing that one exists and that it is happening to you. Most people will readily admit biases exist, but they will not admit that they harbor a bias because admitting this means that we are in some way flawed. Just remember that all humans have biases.

Note the Three Reasons You Have a Bias

There are more than three reasons to have a bias, but these are three ones that are very common.

Strange

The object of your bias is strange to you because you don't really know anything about it and you may have heard negative things about it. You don't really know how many of those stories are true or relevant, but you believe them.

Betrayal

You may be caught up in a group bias and you feel that if you're not biased against whatever the object of your bias is, then you are betraying your group. You feel that you should be prejudiced because everyone else is, and if you're not, then you're weird or wrong.

Attractiveness

Your brain is attracted to this bias because you're not sure if you should really give it up. For example, you may be afraid and biased against those who wear trench coats because the students who committed the heinous crime of murder at Columbine wore trench coats. Therefore, for your own safety, you may feel that you should be afraid of those who wear trench coats because they might be hiding something.

Ask Questions

The third way to rid yourself of a bias is to ask questions about it. Explore the bias. You want to gain insight and lessen the grip that bias has over you. When you feel a bias rising up, ask yourself if it's fair, relevant, or worthy. Ask yourself if it really helps anyone and ask yourself how you obtained this bias. Really explore *why* you're feeling this way instead of immediately running from it.

Not only does this help you avoid biases, it helps you be a happier person when you understand why you feel a certain way and let go of those irrational fears. A bias is nothing more than being irrationally afraid of something or irrationally positive toward something. You're avoiding that bait and trap system that most people are falling into anymore.

Face It

Sometimes the best way we can over a bias is we have to face it with an open mind. This is a lot easier said than done, especially when we have an irrational fear of something. Perhaps you have a bias against a specific nationality or religion, so the best thing you can do is find a place where these people meet up on a regular basis and interact with them. Get to know the people in that room and start looking at them as people rather than as outsiders.

Look for the humanity in the people or the objects. Evaluate your feelings and ask yourself if you're really being rational about what you're thinking or feeling. Then use time to your advantage. Biases will change over time, and it takes time in order for them to change. Take everything slowly.

Take It One Step at a Time

The best thing to do with a bias is to take it one step at a time. You don't want to immerse yourself in what you perceive as wrong or even positive. Step back from it all and really think about it, mull over it. If you know you're being irrational, your bias will be that much easier to overcome.

CHAPTER FIFTEEN:
USE MODELS AND STATISTICS WISELY

When referring to someone who is a professional scientist, what often comes to mind is their focus and dedication to what they are doing. So intense is their focus that often times, scientists are referred to using the term "mad scientist". This term is supposedly to elaborate on their character and intense focus, and the assumption is that they are difficult to communicate with and understand. It is assumed that if you were to speak with them, they would use complex terms, advanced jargon and undiscernible language to explain what they are doing. Once they use these methods to communicate, the result on others is that they may switch off and the message then loses all meaning. This is a situation that applies when people are working with numbers as well. If someone were to try to communicate a mathematical problem to you using a complex formula or specialized methodology, you are unlikely to understand or connect with what is being explained.

Scientific thinking does not revolve around complicated formulas, advanced models and complex statistical methods. However, when one thinks of a scientist, this is what comes to mind. Scientists have long been viewed as geniuses, who are able to understand and explain complex situations by applying knowledge that is not found with the average person. Although there are some attributes that a scientist would have that separates them from other thinkers, the analytical and logical way that they arrive at their conclusions is something that we can all emulate and benefit from.

More often than not, scientific thinking is about following a plan or strategy to arrive at a solution. It is not about complicating a problem and its methodology to the extent that it can no longer be understood. Understanding clues and following steps is what is needed. When explaining a solution, it should be simple enough that the average person can understand the results. This is possible through employing simple diagrams and universal models and statistics to explain conclusions. Simplicity of conclusions also applies when dealing with mathematical problems. Although reaching the solution may entail use of formulas, models and statistics, explaining the methodologies in simple English is normally the right way to form the conclusion of any analysis.

In fact, complicated statistics and methodologies are used when scientists are trying to impress their peers. This is because it is often only their peers who may have any sort of understanding of these methods. Therefore, it can be assumed that use of complex methodologies is not an indication of scientific thinking or reasoning, rather it is a way to explain results and justify "knowledge".

As often happens, some people use complicated methodologies and statistics without fully understanding them or their implications. This is so that they can appear to be forward thinking, intuitive and knowledgeable. When one does not understand their methodologies or the reasons that they are being used, they may produce results that are misleading or even use methodologies that were completely unnecessary. When you are thinking like scientist, especially as you develop your mind to work with numbers, you should learn to appreciate the power of simplicity and logic, versus exaggerating processes and using complex jargon when illustrating your methodologies and conclusions.

However, it is inaccurate to say that you should not use any mathematical models or statistical methods and formulas at all. There is a reason that they are available for analyzing information. The point is to pick relatable methods, formulas or statistics. What you can opt to do is use methods that are easy to understand and interpret, to avoid your work being lost in translation, losing meaning due to wrong methodologies being used, or being rejected due to it being too difficult to understand. There are some universal methodologies that can be used when analyzing information and these include

- Frequency distributions that measure variables against each other to show you the most common occurrences. These are often expressed as a percentage for ease of understanding.

- Standard deviations which shows how measurements within a group are spread out from the average or expected value. This helps you tell how close answers are to the average and therefore how closely they are related to accepted norms.

- Correlations are used to test cause and effect relationships. They can also be used to see whether two variables are associated without having to infer a cause and effect relationship.

- Sample compositions entail being able to assess the population being tested, categorizing them and choosing a representative sample to get a good result.

Among other methods, these are easily recognizable for scientists, mathematicians and the average person. By using this, you can logically arrive at a result by thinking in a step by step fashion. In addition, using these methodologies helps you to illustrate your answers so that the people who are going through them can easily understand the point that you were trying to bring across.

When working mathematically with numbers, it is also important to be able to illustrate your answers so that they can easily be interpreted and understood.

CHAPTER SIXTEEN:
THINK LIKE A MATHEMATICIAN

Thinking like a scientists and thinking like a mathematician are highly related; however, there are a few key differences in the process. You'll still need to follow the basics of thinking logically as if you were a scientist if you're focusing on numbers. In a way, mathematicians are scientists and they access the same base knowledge when they're attempting to solve a problem.

Here are the steps to thinking like a mathematician.

Question Everything

When you're attempting to solve a problem, you want to question all the data that you have in front of you. The beauty of being someone who works with solid numbers and data is that it can all be checked and you don't have to take anyone's word for it when it comes to answers. There's a process known as proving an equation, which can be very simple or complex depending on the equation in question.

The important thing to remember here is that you cannot allow people to feed you information. Your initial reaction to someone's statement should be to automatically disbelieve them until you or they prove otherwise with solid facts and reasoning. Even if the statement turns out to be true, you've mentally exercised your brain to think like a mathematician, which is the ultimate goal.

For example, a letter in a newspaper stated that time travel is not possible because logically, if it were, we would be meeting people from the future already. There are some arguments on both sides of this problem, and it all depends upon what you believe to be logically true. However, a scientists and a mathematician would take all answers into consideration and question them all, as well as their opposites to be sure those are not true.

Write in Sentences

It might seem odd for someone working with numbers to write them down in sentences, but words are the building blocks of an argument. Someone who is a true mathematician and scientists are going to look for more than just an answer, but an answer that is in the form of proof. When you write your answers down in the form of sentences, you are going to think carefully about your answer and may even find mistakes to a seemingly correct answer when you're simply using numbers.

If you're not able to write the sentence fully, then you might not have the correct answer or you might not fully understand what you're writing about. This is an excellent way to develop and expand upon your skills in both mathematics and writing.

Use Converse Statements

Mathematicians and scientists know that they need to use a statement such as A➔B. They know they need to be able to say that if A is true, then B is true. Therefore, the converse statement of A➔B is B➔A.

As an example, you might say that 'If I am George Washington, then I am American' and the converse is 'If I am American, then I am George Washington.'

The second statement is known to be impossible and untrue; therefore, the answer can be 'If I am George Washington, then I am American', but it can't be the converse. A true mathematician and scientist will explore this to sharpen and hone their skills. The question itself is not important, but the process you go through is.

Use Contrapositives

Just like the statement A➔B so B➔A, a contrapositive is A➔B and Not B➔not A. Using the same example, the answers would be 'If I am George Washington, then I am American' and the contrapositive would be 'If I am not Winston Churchill, then I am not English. Unlike a converse statement, a contrapositive statement will always be true if you have the correct answer. It's a good way to double check your work to be sure it's right.

Consider Extreme Examples

Sometimes it's best when we use an extreme example and have a stockpile of them in order to use them when we're working out a problem. Using mundane examples will trigger our minds to think in a mundane manner; therefore, instead of using a number we might use a function instead.

Create Your Own Examples

A mathematician creates their own examples, whether they're extreme or not, because they want to understand the problem inside and out. Sometimes it's easier to work with numbers we're familiar with in the beginning, and then move on to more extreme examples.

Where are Assumptions Used

The hardest part about learning proofs and being a mathematician is understanding that there are assumptions for every proof. You simply have to figure out what those assumptions are and it will help you with the problem better. For example, Pythagoras' Theorem requires the assumption of a right angled triangle. If you don't automatically assume that in that particular proof, then everything you do is going to be for naught. You may see that some proofs refer to another proof, so be sure to check that one for assumptions, too.

Another good tip is to be sure to memorize proofs that are used often. This will help you understand proofs a lot better.

Start with the Complicated

When you're looking at a formula that's very complicated and has two sides, you want to start with the complicated side first and find any substitutions you may be able to make. For example, if you're working with an equation that looks like $A(B+6)=72$, break the equation down into $AB+A6=72$. This is a lot easier to work with when you have to take one part of the equation and add it to another.

Ask What If

When you're working with math, you're working with some assumptions. Ask yourself what would happen if you dropped those assumptions. When you ask questions about what you're doing, you're increasing your understanding and you may even discover a new loophole or an easier way to do something!

Communicate

The best thing you can do when you're trying to learn scientifically or mathematically is communicate with your peers and with your seniors. Always carry a notebook so that you can write down examples and talk with people or ask them to explain something to you. Be aware of what everyone around you is doing and ask them questions when you see them doing something you don't agree with or understand. Collaboration is crucial between scientists and mathematicians, and it's the basic way humans learn.

Now that you know how to think like a scientist and a mathematician, get out there and start talking with your peers!

CONCLUSION

Exercising your brain to think like a scientist involves three things: the ability to pay attention to unexpected findings instead of rejecting them, methodological reasoning and the ability to look beyond a simple answer. When dealing with numbers, it is possible to train the brain towards scientific based goal orientation, whereby, one tries to explain surprising results or inferences from experiments.

Human nature means that we draw on our past experiences and existing knowledge when analyzing and explaining any results. When you choose to think like a scientist, you learn to avoid distorting results by looking for evidence that is consistent with your existing knowledge. Your focus should change to being open to unexpected findings.

Exercise your brain by changing your approach to problems. Rather than viewing problems as a barrier, view them as opportunities that open up for further discovery.

Problem solving should be your focus, rather than avoidance or frustration. If you are working on a problem, and you seem unable to find a solution, identify methods available that will allow you to further analyses the results. To think like a scientist, you should open up your mind to more experiences, and in turn explore methods to build on these experiences.

Remember that the scientist always pursue more than one solution, so evaluate your results in a way that you can get information that represents different points of view.

Exercising your brain will let you reap huge profits from having the right attitude for numbers. It is not so complicated, which you must have figured out after reading this book.

Happy Thinking!

www.ingramcontent.com/pod-product-compliance
Lightning Source LLC
Chambersburg PA
CBHW072143280526
45788CB00002B/759